The Time Before the Secret Words

On the path of Remote Viewing, High Strangeness and Zen

John Vivanco

The Time Before the Secret Words
On the path of Remote Viewing, High Strangeness and Zen

Copyright © 2016 by John Vivanco

john@righthemispheric.com

ISBN-10: 0-9978258-0-4
ISBN-13: 978-0-9978258-0-0

- Fludd's diagram of the mind.

John Vivanco

for Sebastian and Brooke

Acknowledgements

My beautiful, insightful and supportive wife Brooke, who helped guide and edit this project. Being married to her was one of the best decisions I ever made, and I could not have accomplished this without her.

Prudence Calabrese - a best friend, and partner in crime. Through the hardship we endured, the most important thing we did was laugh together.

Mitra-Bishop-Roshi, who talked me out of many trees, and pushed me toward the eye of the needle.

My son Sebastian, who is not only my best buddy, but an amazing Remote Viewer and one of the most intelligent and wittiest individuals I know. I take pride in him being my son.

Of course it goes without saying, thank you to my parents for laying the groundwork on following a more spiritual path without a lot of belief wrapped up in it.

As well, thanks to: Russel Targ, Hal Puthoff, Ingo Swann and all the people responsible for the creation of the Remote Viewing protocol. I believe it was a gift to the world no matter how much I soapbox on the military intelligence apparatus which still lurks behind it. Thanks to Linda and Howie Kaufman for helping when I needed it and to all the Remote Viewers I have trained and worked with.

Introduction

We move like ghosts through the ether, silent and undetectable, gathering information that can't be gathered any other way. To Al Qaeda, we are of the Djinn; to the FBI, we are Psychic Spies.

When the Twin Towers fell, we were likely part of some Hail Mary plan the FBI had -- "break glass in case of major terrorist attack only". They knew about us because we had run slightly afoul of them on a treasure hunting project, then again, every intelligence service knew of us. We were a successful Civilian Remote Viewing think tank developed just after it became declassified.

Post 9/11, the FBI brought us in to Remote View future terrorist attacks, and we were successful in helping to prevent another. The odd thing was, even though we were helping prevent terrorist attacks, there was a secretive covert group whose sole job was to shut us down. From setups, to death threats, we dodged as much as we could so we could keep working to bring this amazing ability to the world.

Being a Remote Viewer can also result in an exorbitant amount of High Strangeness. It opens the door to mind-bending projects which force you to see the world in a completely different light. One moment you're working on predicting markets for a hedge fund, the next, you're an inadvertent contact point to an alien species asking you for help.

I didn't arrive at Remote Viewing with the belief I had any psychic ability at all. It was, in fact, the words of Mr. Causey ultimately driving me. As a child, he warned me to always remember the time before words – the moment before thought is created. This obsession sent me on a journey to explore my consciousness and to know the self, where it left me to live in a Zen Center, while running a team of Remote Viewers.

.
.
.
.
.
.
.
.

What is that moment before thoughts are created?

the televised event; a sold out sporting venue and a terror spectacle designed for maximum fear.

As he jumped and tumbled from the tiered seating down toward the playing field, people scrambled and parted as much as they could. The pop pop sound of the fold out seats hitting the backrests as the terror began. Gravity pulling him down and down, a horrific gas cloud chased him and spread to the bottlenecked spectators. There was no way of getting away from it, and those it hit first began to foam at the mouth and convulse in the concrete aisles, setting off an even more massive wave of panic.

It was the blindside by a citizen, and the fall to the stadium field that knocked his gas mask loose and jarred his brain. As he fell, the Samaritan fell, a useless noble effort because the gas was escaping with full force. In fact, there was nothing anyone could do, except run. The canisters will bleed dry until they can no more, regardless if the carrier is dead or alive.

On the field he ran, people parting and scattering, then dropping. As his momentum slowed and the control of his seizing body became impossible, he tried to find a place near the vents to gas out, die, and conclude a successful operation. He only made it so far as the tunnel where the players of the teams came running out to the playing field. The thick, cool, concrete walls, like a massive cave drew him in where he sat down on the ground, propped himself against the wall, and mumbled "Allahu Akbar", as his body shook and collapsed into death.

Many miles away, another event was taking place around the same time. A lone canister is dropped through a dislodged vent which leads to a system of air circulation in an underground area full of trains and people. The New York City subway. As it descends, the canister begins to release its deadly aerosol into the venting system. Tiny cells floating in an ether, multiplying and replicating. Coming to rest, it sprays, sputters and stops. The large cloud trails and drifts into a fan where it's sucked into a venting system that feeds the platforms where the people wait. It's a vehicle for a biological pathogen and it has released its payload.

At the same time, multitudes of people are draining from a concert at Madison Square Garden, heading down into the subway to make their way to varied destinations. As they stand in the hot zone waiting, with each unaware inhalation, each unaware person is breathing in this disease and becoming a carrier.

The first tier of exposure is seen within a week. Pustulating red mounds cover their bodies, with stomach cramps and bleeding ulcers in the mouth and throat. All this is accompanied by high fevers and the inability to cogitate clearly or barely even move. Many people die from this pox and it carries itself into an uncertain future for years to come.

The worst of all of this was yet to arrive, and behind the scenes it set law enforcement into a frenzied panic with the belief it would unfold at any moment. Suitcase nukes on US soil, and in control of an Al Qaeda associated group. If one were approached and apprehended, the others would detonate.

But, none of this had happened yet.

I am a trained psychic spy, a Remote Viewer, hired by the FBI to remote view future terrorist attacks. These were some of the events we perceived through this method of information collection - a multi-pronged attack with a sporting event at the center. Our team, a civilian think tank, was pulled into the world of counter-terror shortly after 9/11.

As I sat there frozen, the possibilities racing in my mind, I began to feel tremors course through me. Waves of physical shaking as the visuals from the remote viewing data were left echoing in my head. It's not like you can just erase what you've seen and felt within remote viewing sessions, but I have to get past it at the moment. With too much work to do and too many reports to finish, I had to cut out of a meditation retreat for this. I live in a Zen Center with its peaceful atmosphere, yet I am showing signs of PTSD.

In reality, the PTSD wasn't just from this current terrorist related work. I was already looking over my shoulder. Over the years our remote viewing team had been hounded, harassed, and threatened with death by a mysterious group, and at this moment, it was all taking its toll.

CHAPTER TWO

Remote Viewing Beginnings

Have you ever wanted to travel the Universe with your mind? Hell, did it ever cross your mind? What if you could move forward or backward in time, taking notes, grabbing images and building pictures of what occurred, what's occurring, and what is yet to come? What if you could know what is at any location on Earth, Mars, the Moon, or anywhere else in the Universe without having to go there physically?

The US government sure wanted to know, and they developed a program to explore if this was a feasible way to collect information. No technology, just the human mind.

In the late 1960's and early 1970's it came through the US intelligence grapevine the Soviet Union was developing psychics as spies. With an apparent program already in place, the US decided to play catch up - so the story goes.

Some of the thinking may have been; you can't have your sworn enemy doing something you're not doing, even if you think it's nuts. Then again, it does absolve some of the collective shame for shoveling millions of dollars into a dirty word: "psychic phenomena". "We thought it was stupid from the beginning, but they started it!" Beyond that though, people in power have used "seers" and "oracles" since the dawn of man, no matter what the public thinks of it. This is just the bureaucratized version.

The CIA tasked physicist Dr. Hal Puthoff with looking into whether psychics could be used as an intelligence-gathering tool, and shortly thereafter he brought in another physicist, Russel Targ. Both scientists were based out of Stanford University in Palo Alto California, where they conducted their cutting-edge scientific work under the company name of SRI International.

Originally formed by Stanford University in the 1940's, SRI conducts brainy research and development on the very fringes of human scientific understanding. Having many military and government contracts during the "revolutionary" 1960's, it was akin to consorting with the enemy, so they cut it loose to stand on its own as an individual company responsible for itself. SRI International still exists to this day, receiving funding on government related projects, and even though Targ and Puthoff played a large role in the Institute after it was cut loose, they have been thoroughly scrubbed from the current website and there is no mention of them or Remote Viewing.

Both men were PhD's - accomplished laser physicists before they became involved in psychic investigations for SRI. Puthoff was well known for his work on zero point energy and quantum vacuum states, along with inventing the tunable infra-red laser. By the time Targ had joined, his list of inventions were the tunable plasma oscillator, the high-power gas-transport laser, and the FM laser. Both men had an interest in psychic functioning, and had conducted their own investigations in this realm prior to any contact with the CIA. As far as Putoff was concerned, this was the reason they wanted him heading up the investigation, and they gave him eight months to accomplish it.

One of the first test subjects was the Israeli psychic and spoon-bender, Uri Geller, but it wasn't until they brought in Ingo Swann that the program started to achieve tangible results. A New York based artist as well as a "consciousness researcher" with natural psychic abilities, he never took part in these experiments as merely a test subject, but as one who was also crafting them.

Aside from the, "tell me what I've hidden

in the box" experiments, they had to be developed in a meaningful way for espionage, so the psychic didn't burn out. Ingo, having come from the "test subject" side, knew this and worked with SRI to create more involved and creative experiments, but the biggest issue by far was one of repeatability.

At the time, most parapsychology researchers and institutes had come to the conclusion that repeatable results would never be attained. If they couldn't get past that stage, the deal was over. Through all the testing and experiments, they only had two models which could possibly make the cut, but they both had big issues.

One, was to give a Remote Viewer the name of a location to remote view, but this method gives the Viewer too much information. Because of critics, and basic methods and controls in the research, the test subject must not be cued in any way, so it meant they could not use this as a means of intelligence gathering.

The second method utilized a person called an Outbounder. This person would head off to a predetermined location, unknown to the Viewers, which was randomly chosen from a stack of envelopes. During the time the Outbounder was waiting at the location, Remote Viewers in a lab would begin describing where this person was. Acting as a beacon to break through the muck of the psychics' minds, the

Outbounder scenario was successful, but could not be used for espionage purposes either. Sending an "agent" to a secret location they wanted information on is not feasible for a covert CIA operation. Whatever they created, it had to stand on its own.

With the clock ticking, they were up against the wall. If funding died, Ingo would head back to New York and an uncertain monetary future. A most unpleasant thought, and one that drove him to get focused.

With a bottle of scotch, he headed to the apartment complex pool in Menlo Park, where he was renting for the duration of the experiments. His only task - bob in the pool, drink the bottle, and come up with the solution.

Floating in the water half the night and sipping scotch, he came to a point where he was too wasted to survive floating any longer, and headed to the edge of the pool. Uncertainly clutching the side, blurry eyed, but still holding the question - I guess you could say it finally hit him. A disembodied voice told him, "try coordinates". By this, the voice meant Earth coordinates you find on a map. Often times drunk ideas only sound best when you're drunk, but this was exactly what he needed, the "address" to send a Remote Viewer to. Since there are millions of coordinates across the Earth, there was no way a Remote Viewer could "cheat".

Targ and Puthoff were initially against testing this idea, but not for the fear that it would waste precious time and resources by not working. They were apprehensive because they may not be able to explain how this worked from a physics standpoint, but in the face of trying to create the fantastic, it kind of becomes a moot point.

Ultimately, it worked. The success of using this method proved to be what they needed, and once demonstrated to the CIA, they were fully on board. Ingo was credited with the idea of Controlled Remote Viewing, and it became the basis for the protocol we use today.

The methodology was implemented within, and for, the US Intelligence services. Calling it many code names through the years, it ended with Stargate, and it was their job to supply requested intelligence information to other agencies through the method of Remote Viewing. In a sense, intelligence agencies would "place orders" and the Stargate Remote Viewers would work them.

In 1995 the Stargate project was declassified by the CIA under the assertion it was being abandoned because of a lack of applicable uses. They issued a document called the AIR Report which was researched and written by two people -- a skeptic and a believer. The final report was half-ass and skewed to show the program was unsuccessful, and the methodology used to determine this left out interviews with key people and 80% of the successful missions. It was a manipulated and doomed report from the beginning, regardless of how successful remote viewing was.

Through my years of working in the remote viewing field, I have come to realize it lives a healthy life beyond the declassification of the Stargate program. The AIR report was just meant for public consumption because of embarrassing leaks around it, and those within intelligence know it works. There was the declassified Stargate, but how many other agencies picked up the protocol and ran with it on their own?

Remote viewing opens an individual to a whole new way of perceiving and a whole new world. Your definition of reality changes and expands into worlds you never knew existed. It's not just what occurs in individual sessions either. When you run projects with multiple Remote Viewers all viewing the same thing - the same question - you are able to paint a very coherent picture of just about anything, and this is the real power within the protocol.

Because of my past, and experiences with the exploration of my consciousness and Zen, I suppose it was natural I get pulled into the world of remote viewing. The one thing I didn't know was the road it would lead me down. For someone who was completely unconnected with any military apparatus, the danger of turning this into a business became apparent rather quickly.

The other side of this is the High Strangeness aspect, which rears its head when you go deep in this field. The opening of the mind to the mysteries of the Universe is one thing, but when it arrives and sits on your couch, your world view completely changes.

But by far, the greatest place it helped me reach was the realization that remote viewing and Zen are one in the same. A perfect convergence point which can open you up to yourself in order to perceive the true nature of reality.

CHAPTER THREE
Mr. Causey and the Bell

Circa – Teen/Childhood

It was the sound of the reverberating church bell that prompted me to pass out. A wavering stereo-chorus wrapping around the sound of a bell, bouncing in my ears until it triggered something long forgotten. I don't remember what my body was doing at that moment, other than a feeling of total coordination loss. It was likely this whole vision occurred as I was crumpling in a slow drift to the floor.

The jolt of the sound on my senses transported me to another time and place. In this vision, I was staring at a large cross propped up on a wall made of dried mud with a sensation of fresh death all around me. It must be a combination of smell and feeling, but a sickly sweet and bitter cloud of death covered the area, and as I spun around, a horrible scene lay before me of piles of people killed. Somehow I knew this was done by "the church". Somehow I knew this was an inquisition.

The man against the wall was wearing a brown sackcloth robe with a rope tied around his waist like a belt. A priest. He was me. I did not know how this was possible at that moment, but I knew somehow, it was me. The priest slowly dropped to his knees with his hands over his face, and I knew he was about to be killed. Before I could see the event unfold, I uncontrollably came ripping back to the now.

When I awoke from this, my face was pressed against the carpet and my eyes were trying to focus. The angle was different from before I collapsed. My friend was now sideways in my vision and was staring at me perplexed. As I pushed myself up from the carpet, his finger was still perched over the keyboard creating the sound, but the wavering bell was no more.

He asked me what happened, but I couldn't think in words or relay anything with any coherency. I was still lost in the feeling of death. To my teenage mind it was a bit of a problem - it's kind of a snag when all you really want is for people to think you're cool, so I said nothing.

What did all of that mean? Why did I see that? How could I be me and someone else? But, the biggest concern I had at that moment was, was this a precursor to my death? Was I going to die soon?

Right on the heels of this, a strange and distant thread of a memory came winding back from the age of three or four (sometime during early 1970's). There was no outward connection between them, but I knew it must somehow be related.

In this memory, there was a rush of water flowing down the street next to the curb, while I was busy pushing my plastic baseball bat through the water on my hands and knees. The gushing of water was infinitely pleasant as my fake "All-American" bat caught the water and caused it to spray on me.

As if out of nowhere, a man was suddenly standing next to me.

My eyes traveled up from his beaten black wing tips, to the heavy brown wool suit with the wide 1970's collar and the pee-yellow shirt. He had big, thick black framed glasses, a mop of brown hair and bushy mustache making him look like Groucho Marx. The air around him was depressed, like the wool suit was forever weighing him down. In one hand he carried a leather briefcase, and as I watched him, his other hand slowly lifted and pointed up the street.

I followed the pointing finger to a man in a driveway, who had a car engine hoisted in the air. He was using a hose and solvents to clean it as it hung there, dripping grease and chemicals into the flow of the water that I was playing in. I looked back to the wool suit man while he turned around and moped away.

I wasn't sure, but I thought I was in trouble, so I ran inside the house.

It had to have been a couple weeks after that first visit, when I began to notice I had an internal voice. I called the voice, my "secret words". Words no one else can hear. Words I create. This was obviously the beginning of another level of thought and my understanding of how to begin to use it. It's the moment I began to conceptualize the world around me and live in my head rather than the pure experience of what is unfolding, as children do. During the time this was developing, I encountered him again.

As I was playing in my bedroom, experimenting with these words, he showed up with the same briefcase and the same suit. He said he could hear my secret words and so could the others who lived where he lived. He also said I am hearing his secret words right now, as it's all he speaks in. He said his name was Mr. Causey and he was a traveling accountant who died from a heart attack.

To my child mind it was just taken in

stride, and I had no idea about ghosts or Spirit Guides. I felt he was nice man, if not a little boring, depressed, and in a hurry. In fact he told me all he did was travel, but he would check in on me from time to time and say hello. Before he left, he imparted one thing that stuck in my child mind. He said I should always remember the time before the secret words.

I never thought to mention it to my parents, but when I finally spoke about Mr. Causey, they called him my imaginary friend. Who has an imaginary friend who is a depressed traveling accountant? I would have created someone with amazing superpowers, or at the very least, someone who would play with me. He was a perpetual traveling accountant, always looking for the perfect number, not someone who wanted to play dinosaurs.

When the remembrance crawled to the forefront of my brain, after the vision from the bell, I knew somehow it was important, but it only left me with more questions. How could I be me and the priest, and what does it mean to "remember the time before the secret words"? Worst of all though, was the calm confusion I felt, mixed with the panic of looming death.

John Vivanco

CHAPTER FOUR
1995 – The Declassification

Ted Koppel; America's friendly uncle, the man you have no problem believing whatever he tells you. He seems to be a fair and balanced individual, able to look at both sides and relay information truthfully, so when news broke and remote viewing rose from the dark vaults of secrecy, he was there to begin the fair outing of it on Nightline. He said it was a failure, but somewhere deep inside I knew there was more to the story.

Before I could get to that point though, I had to deal with my inner 10 year old boy upon hearing the term "psychic spy". An immediate eye twitch and repetitive mumbling of psychic spy, I could only think within the context of a pre-teen boy... "they're real life superheroes! Ok, I have to do that". I wish I could I say I knew right then and there I had to do this because it was something that could change the world and how we perceive it, but I think the fact I had a dead traveling accountant for an "imaginary friend" was a complete set-up to always want to go the route of the garishly fantastic.

For whatever reason, some people seem to be attraction points for paranormal and psychic happenings, and I have to admit on occasion I would be one as well. Overall though, early incidents seemed to send me in pointed directions as opposed to a haphazard paranormal beat. It was more my personality to go against the grain and rebel, and remote viewing fit neatly within that construct. It seemed to me, you could know literally anything with this, and I had to learn it.

There was scant Internet back then, but I still fired up my "blazingly fast", yet slightly disappointing, 33k modem to see what I could find. It was actually surprising I even had a computer. As a kid my Dad bought a few throughout the years, but that was before there was an Internet. In the 80's he connected through a service called CompuServe, which triggered a "rise of the robots" fear in my Mom's mind. Every time that dial-up modem sound occurred, she would share with us kids a lecture or two on these robot wars. "Computers will take us over and destroy us one day. Be prepared - they are going to kill us all!!!" To this day, the ancient sound of the modem as it begins to connect brings fear and trepidation. I, for one, am happy we don't have to listen to that anymore.

When I checked online, there was a small ex-military crowd already teaching remote viewing for the exorbitant fee of way more than I could afford for a simple weekend course. Some of them were as high as $12,000, and my newly completed degree in fine art didn't afford me a lot of luxuries. The only thing I could do was monitor and research, hoping to gain a little sliver of information on how to do it.

Persistence paid off and it wasn't too long after, I began to find snippets on how to do it. With a word here and a word there, I could begin to understand how this process worked, enough to begin to try in a limited way. Then I hit pay dirt, I found a manual online, and the moment began where I really started to learn.

Different protocols exist for Remote Viewing with names like Controlled Remote Viewing (CRV), Technical Remote Viewing (TRV), Extended Remote Viewing (ERV), Scientific Remote Viewing (SRV), etc... no matter what anyone tells you, they are just derivatives of each other, and all the same at the base level. Remote viewing is just a protocol in order to exercise and repeat the inherent psychic functioning we all have. Even the hardened skeptic, I can guarantee you, has had at least one moment in their life where they had a 6th sense;

a gut feeling. Remote viewing allows you to begin to corral this, increase it, and repeat it.

Unleashing remote viewing to the masses brought a tear to the eye of many civilians. UFO investigators and enthusiasts, as well as an assorted number of conspiracy theorists, could begin to use a tool to deepen their understanding, and perhaps find the truth of nearly anything. Like a virgin on their wedding night, this community began to remote view every single conspiracy there ever was, and ever will be. There was a lot of "everything is something" at that time.

With a very large following, one group claimed they had remote viewed Martians underneath Santa Fe Baldy in New Mexico. Apparently transported there quite some time ago by Grey aliens in order to save them from the desolation of their home planet. Word from the Remote Viewers though - they were on the verge of starvation and hunger with their supplies running out fast. Some of the Internet message boards were trying to figure out how to find them so they could deliver food and water - a canned food drive for the Martians.

Then there was the unfortunate Hale-Bopp comet fiasco, where the Farsight Institute remote viewed an anomalous object in the tail of the comet. There were numerous reports and photos from amateur astronomers of this mystery object, and this piqued their interest to look into it. Later, they even received a roll of negatives from a University Astronomer of the anomaly and worked many Remote Viewing projects around those photos - from what it is, to who it is, and where it was going. They published all their analysis on the object, even going so far as being interviewed on radio programs. In the midst of this, it was claimed the astronomer photos were faked, and The Farsight Institute was dragged through the mud.

None of it turned out well for anyone, except possibly the Remote Viewing disinformation team assigned to the operation.

If this was the case, part of the intended blow back from this would be the self-policing of the Remote Viewing community. In other words, loud voices who shame those remote viewing projects of an unverifiable nature - projects that you cannot confirm whether the RV data is correct or not physically. They will often point to this event as proof you should not do it... because you could be wrong, it's subject matter for the crazies, and you should only work on completely verifiable targets to convince the world Remote Viewing is real.

At a very basic level, remote viewing is a threat to a power structure and all its secrets. By creating a situation where Remote Viewers shame each other from looking at these, well, mission accomplished - hypothetically of course. As a government who still believes in remote viewing, they would have to control where it goes after declassification. It would be critical to manipulate the newly forming community so they don't get too deep into things they should not know about.

A quick note on remote viewing nomenclature -- most of the remote viewing community calls what they view a "target", this implies separation i.e. there is you, and then there is something else, but you could not remote view if this were truly the case. Another implication is that you want to shoot it, i.e., target. Therefore I do not use the word "target" when I refer to what the Remote Viewer views, because to me it is inherently misleading. I use the word, "objective" as a replacement. When you see that word from here on out, you will know I am referring to what a Remote Viewer views, and it's the same as what everyone else in the RV world calls a "target". As well, the term "remote viewing" is misleading, but I will save that discussion for another time!

With a lot of protocol to absorb and keep in the forefront of my mind, I stumbled through the first "real" session I did. Twenty different wrong conclusions were scrawled across my papers, but in between these there were real edges of information poking through. I would quickly sense things like a tank track, the color green, a diesel exhaust smell and the sense of flags or nationalism. They were like ghosts in the way they came and went quickly, slipping through so fast, that if I wasn't paying attention, I would miss it. It turns out, that first objective was a subject in China standing in front of a row of tanks during the Chinese democratic revolution; the Tiananmen Square Tank Guy.

The obvious point for me after doing a few became how the conceptualizing mind wants to get involved with trying to "guess" what it is, but it's rarely if ever correct, and it clouds the real information trying to come through. I was learning you have to stay, what I call low-level, and just describe things, not name things. The naming of things is much different than just describing, and that "naming" can create poor sessions.

Remote viewing was, and still is, populated by ex-military intelligence types training the interested, so I was conflicted how to receive it formally. In my mind, you never retire when you have that status in the military and I wasn't sure if I wanted to go that route.

Prudence Calabrese, or Pru to her friends, worked for the Farsight Institute and had become a reluctant voice for the group because of her experiences with what she describes as a small Grey Alien. The "Grey Dude", as she called him, would show up in her bathroom around 2am many nights where she would be hypnotically pulled from sleep to receive a mental message. Like an intricately tied knot, many of these thought-balls would have to be carefully unraveled to reveal the details. Overall, they were related to many things affecting a small circle of people, to the larger universe.

Aside from her paranormal and strange experiences, she was very down to earth with no overt military connections. A very intelligent woman, her immediate background had been in the scientific field, developing cyclotrons, so she had a very analytical and intuitive approach to everything she did. As well, she had a deep desire for digging into strange phenomena, and being a Buddhist meditation practitioner herself, I felt an alignment with her. When she broke with the Farsight Institute after the Hale Bopp fiasco it was my chance to get trained more formally.

The first class I took was at a dingy hotel conference room in San Diego with stains on the carpet smelling of the year 1971. The yellow curtains cast a perpetual sunset, so I constantly yawned. It was like an old meet-up location for worn out detectives and depleted prostitutes, which was the perfect back drop to learn it, except for the yawning. Come to think of it, a bit more of a sci-fi background would have been nice. The setting was more in line with a, "how to use microfiche machines" workshop. Nonetheless, I was already training myself prior to this, so it wasn't too much about learning it; it was about working with other people and going deeper.

In remote viewing, especially starting out,

you need someone to give you objectives so that you, as the Viewer, remain "blind" (not knowing what the objective is). Once you get pulled into a system, the instructor should have something set up in order to provide continual practice for students, and that she did. I began getting tasked by Pru and sending her my sessions for comment and continued training.

My Fine Art degree meant I was classically trained in drawing and painting, which in turn means, I describe how light falls on a surface. Really though, it's all just fancy talk for: I describe things physically and realistically. It doesn't mean I draw beautifully detailed pictures when remote viewing, rather, it means I have a propensity to see the world that way, and is related in my sessions.

We all have filters within our perceptions. We experience through concepts, metaphors, similes, illustrative examples, and on and on. If you take a writer for example, one who is trained to see and describe through concepts and metaphors, then you are going to have someone with a completely different way of looking at the world which will reflect within their sessions. Every single Remote Viewer, just like every human, has a unique way of describing the world around them, and because my leanings were on the physical side, its value didn't go unnoticed.

Soon after this class, Pru had completely cut from the Farsight Institute and moved to the

Carlsbad area in San Diego County, California. When she left, some of the Remote Viewers from the Institute went along with her in order to work on projects she was directing, and that's when I got invited to attend a short weekend training course at her house with these "operational" Remote Viewers.

During the practice sessions on the first day, there were palpable sensations which were quite cool and very "on", but nothing spectacular overall. It was just a continuation of my expansion and deeper understanding of the SRV protocol. Later that night though, a bout of high strangeness came on.

At the time I lived up in Orange County, near LA, and it was easier to stay at her place without having to drive home in the evening, and back in the morning. She had a couple of young boys who were staying with their father that weekend so I was given the top of their bunk bed to sleep in.

Strange house, strange bed, and my frame not fitting in the small bunk bed so well, I slept off and on throughout the night. Around 2am I was pulled from a semi-conscious state gagging on the most horrific smell you could imagine. It was a mix of citrus and old rotten dirty diapers all twirled into one single scent, but that only begins to hint at the deathly smell. It was as though someone had the bright idea of placing a month's worth of dirty diapers and garbage in a warm humid closet, then tried to cover it up with an orange scented spray. Pure death and a sorry association with something that smells good.

I recalled Pru saying the Grey who comes to visit smells just like that, and 2am was the witching hour where he would come relieve himself of a message in her bathroom. The damn smell was so bad I figured it had to be in the room with me. If it was an attempt to cover up his native smell with an orange scented spray, then kudos to him! Thank you for trying.

The unfortunate choice I had at that moment was to either pull the covers over my head and hide from the potential of him and the reality of the smell, or see what I can see. Decisions, decisions... Not sleeping so well in the first place, it wasn't like I could just brush it off.

When I was around 19, I moved in with a girlfriend who was going to a University in San Diego. She and some roommates rented a suburban house on a suburban street near the University, and I became good friends with one roommate's boyfriend, Nick. He would stay there most of the time and we would hang out, drink, play music and generally get in trouble. One day I arrived home and noticed a book on the kitchen table. On the cover of the book was an artist's rendition of a Grey alien with its large oblong head and almond shaped eyes. The book was called Communion by Whitley Strieber.

At that point in time I had not heard of "Grey Aliens", nor did I give the idea of aliens any thought at all. It was something which had no reason to enter into my consciousness, so I had no clue what this book was about.

As I looked at the book cover and the face, an inexplicable fear tore through my whole being, and I wanted to hide. I remembered right then, they *were* somehow a real thing, even though I had no context for it. All I could really piece together at the moment were these brief snippets full of panic, fear and struggle while I was pulled through my bedroom window by them. Whenever that would happen, I would later find myself outside the house in a field next door, having to find a way back inside and back to bed. I never spoke of it to my parents because it was something that lingered on the edge of consciousness and made it easy to step around mentally. It just didn't make any sense.

As much as I didn't want to know anything about it, my friend explained it anyway, and he also spoke of his experiences being "taken". I wanted nothing to do with it even though it brought some context to those unexplained happenings in my early life. I also tried to stay away from those things in my head afterward, but unfortunately I couldn't. They started to take me again at that time and after.

So, the big question - did I really want to pull myself to the edge of the bunk bed to see what was happening in the room with me? It was a reluctant hell yeah! I have always been one who wants to push the red button.

I tried to be very very quiet as I did this, as though I could be completely invisible and quieter than a ninja. I really wasn't interested in getting taken again. Problem is, it's a tall wooden structure I am on which shakes and rubs and squeaks when you move, and it did all that as if it were in the Olympics of shaking, rubbing and squeaking!

So I just lurched to edge of the damn bed, look straight down, and there was nothing there but toys the kids had been playing with before they left.

As I sat there rigid and alert, my eyes scanned across the floor to the bedroom doorway when my heart started to race even faster. It was a bit lighter in the hallway, just outside the bedroom door, and that's where I saw him.

Standing in the doorway, more of a shadow than anything else, yet with his big head and small, thin body, he lingered as if contemplating whether he needed to do something right then. I really didn't want to go through the window, get dumped outside and then end up knocking on the door in the early morning trying to explain why I'm outside. Although Pru would probably understand, and I could just say it how it is. Pru: "Why are you out there at 3am John?!" Me: "Abducted". Pru: "Aliens are just a bunch of punk ass bitches". You would think if they could pull you out of a window, they can put you back in that window. Lazy bastards.

So I held my breath waiting for the inevitable, when he suddenly disappeared. It felt like a close call, and I was still waiting for him to come back as the smell dissipated. I figured he was truly gone after the scent left, and so I finally let myself relax and fall asleep.

CHAPTER FIVE
The Forming Path

I was baptized Catholic, presumably as an insurance policy from going to hell, but my parents were the occasional pot smoking, Che Guevara-loving hippies, and we never ever went to any church.

My Father was from Chile, had grown up within archaic Catholic schools, and had very devout parents. I am sure in the back of his head he heard the priest admonishing him for not baptizing us kids, and that was his reasoning. Better to be safe than sorry.

The years of my mom's youth on the other hand, was one of heavy smokers and alcoholic parents, but that was quite normal for the time. The 50's and 60's in the US was a time of high-functioning alcoholics like my Grandfather.

Being business partners with the famous inventor, Dr. Arnold Beckman, he owned a glass instrument company, and was more the scientific and practical type. When my mom was in high school, she decided she needed religion of some sort and went to a Protestant church, where she would attend regularly and alone. Her intention through this was an exploration of herself, but she decided it could only take her so far, so it didn't last long.

Expansion of the mind and thinking for yourself, outside of any religion, was their ultimate route, which they instilled in me. Eastern philosophy, primarily Zen, was something they began to follow when I was young. Zen doesn't have much of a belief system, it is simply a meditation practice so you can find the answers within yourself. Occasionally when we were kids my Dad would give my brother, sister, and I, a couple bucks if we could meditate on a cushion for about five minutes. It's a great way to play the "silent game" and shut the kids up... "meditate and gain enlightenment kids, plus, earn a bit of cash in the process!".

I perceived high school as a complete waste of time. I balked at the authority and what I thought to be useless adventures in what and how I should learn. When I was interested and applied myself I got A's, other than that, I used my intellect to figure out ways to ditch school without getting in trouble. I wanted out as fast as I could, because I wasn't interested in this system. My parents were somewhat dismayed because my brother and sister were model students, heading off to college. Returning to the horror of formal education was too much for me to recreate, so instead of college, I immersed myself in writing music, playing in bands and working odd jobs.

The biggest issue I faced were a mess of conflicting feelings, and that was the driving factor for what I did. The bell and the resulting vision of someone who is you, but not you, then dies, is rather confusing. It gave me a sense of "who cares; I'm going to die soon, so I'll do what I want". But I couldn't be completely free within that because, attached to it, were the words of Mr. Causey. I was frustratingly stuck somewhere in the middle, wanting to explode into complete "who cares", yet restrained by needing to know who I was, and what comes before the "secret words". It almost felt like a deep sense of responsibility I carried, which held me back from going too far on the side of not giving a shit.

This drew me into the futilistic ideas within Existentialist philosophy. In particular, I was caught up in the sensation, confusion and depression that it was all meaningless; the dead end of Existentialism. I couldn't even think about building a future, because I didn't believe I had one, so I just worked on the expression of it through music and bands.

Subconsciously, I wanted to get beyond

this point, to see something deeper, but I was just left hanging by conscious mental constructs of what life is and meant.

The vision from the bell and the words of Mr. Causey drifted off deep into my psyche, because they didn't solve the practicality of surviving moment to moment. Instead what took hold was a longing, a gut wrenching feeling I had to get back to something, but that something was more unknown than known. The thing is, life takes turns almost unknowingly to our conscious minds, and experiences come to us based on the deep yearnings we have.

How many people end up looking for answers in writings and what others have to say? I was doing just that, reading ideas of others to find an answer, and it was going nowhere. At a certain point it began to dawn on me, I would get nothing from any book or thought in my head. Nothing would tell me what this moment was, and nothing would tell me who I was or relieve the suffering I was feeling. It all had to come from within me. I felt a deep and expanding pit of emptiness inside, consuming all my waking moments. It felt uncomfortable and painful, like something was eating away at me from the depths of my being; eating all my ideas and challenging my sense of self.

I wanted to try something different so I stopped reading these books, filling my head with ideas and decided to turn inward for answers, so I shifted my energy to meditation.

I would watch my breath and count as it went in and out, in and out, one through ten and ten to one. I would try hard to keep my thoughts from wandering and try not to berate myself when I was caught in random thoughts the whole time sitting there. It's difficult when the habit established is to experience everything through thought, but I wanted to experience from somewhere else. I tried for a while but it didn't seem to do much. I felt calmer, but overall I still struggled with the deepening pit in my stomach and this sense that life was completely worthless.

What happened after a couple months of this was quite unexpected.

I was working as a security guard at a very wealthy gated community in the San Diego area. It was the normal routine, no construction traffic could come into the community before 7am so they would all line up just outside the gate waiting. Occasionally one would try and sneak in before the proper time.

I was the gatekeeper and no one would get in on my watch. It was probably around 6:30 in the morning and an El Camino, green, rusty and looking like it came straight out of the 70's rolled up to the guard booth I was sitting in. I stared at the guy behind the window, waiting for him to roll it down so I could tell him he can't get in yet, and he has to go back out onto the street to wait another half an hour.

As his window came down, he looked up at me and I explained the situation. "Look Buddy..." As the words came out of my mouth slower and slower; as the words trailed - "you can't... come......... in............ till.....................
7:00", his eyes shone at me with some kind of fun but mirthful questioning. Not one word came out of his mouth, just staring with a look filled with light and questioning.

In that moment I seemed to grab an edge of the absurdity of time, rules, definitions, structures, and thoughts we create around everything. I immediately understood the depression I had was a structure I was creating. I was responsible, and could create it, or not create it. It was up to me and not what life is, or isn't. It most definitely was not what someone else was telling me! In one instant a whole mental construct I was creating and living in, completely fell to pieces.

The 7am rule was just the same, and I started laughing, and laughing. It was hilarious! So I let him in much to the dismay of the other guards in the booth with me. I was crawling out of the self-imposed hole of depression based on the feelings from all the ideas I created.

This event changed the way I perceived things. It launched me into a place of understanding that no books or information would take me to. In fact the books just created thoughts that got in the way of being and fully experiencing. From there I knew, in order to know anything of value, it had to come from within me, and Zen meditation was the route.

John Vivanco

CHAPTER SIX
Two Weeks

"All I want you to do is go to the front door and step outside!" My monitor was clearly frustrated with me, as I spent the better part of an hour bouncing back and forth between two aspects of an objective that was going nowhere.

I was perceiving a house on fire with a subject (a person) acting franticly inside. Walls, furniture, household items, all in flames. Quite suddenly, when I probed for a different aspect of this scenario, I would find myself within a metallic structure with girders running the length. Another subject was here busying with maps, data, and looking through various types of scopes and instruments. I could not reconcile these seemingly different aspects, and my monitor wanted me to.

"Ok", I said, "Let me do a movement

exercise." As my monitor suggested, I wrote down on my paper, "Go to door, step outside and describe".

My monitor and I were sitting on a couch with other Remote Viewers around the room, each with their own monitor, and each working on a RV session. The job of a monitor is to keep the Viewer on task and urge them to expand their data where needed - another aspect of remote viewing people are trained in. Even though I had already been trained by Pru previous to this, I was invited to take part in a two week intensive on remote viewing at her house.

As I settled my mind and closed my eyes in order to do the movement exercise my monitor instructed me to do, I also stood up from the couch as if to mimic a person walking to a door and turning the knob. This seemed to trigger something, this mimicking of movement in a session, because the moment I did it, I began to feel as though my whole body was on fire.

When I closed my eyes, I suddenly had what is called a bi-location event. A whole scene came in to full focus behind my eyes, and I was able to move around at will within this vision as if I were completely there. Bi-location is a phenomena that occurs to Remote Viewers and psychics at times, when you are suddenly in two places at once; in your normal every day body and in another location elsewhere. It is said, you can also show up in a physical way at this remote location when it occurs, to the point that other people there can see you.

In Pru's living room, with other Remote Viewers involved with their own sessions, I began to semi-run in place as I saw all around me a nighttime city on fire. With the burning sensations cutting into me, I began running down a street of this ancient city with a sea of flame engulfing everything. I realized where I was and began screaming - "I am in Dresden, I am on fire! I am in Dresden, I am on fire!!!"

As I opened my eyes, back to the living room I was in, everyone was staring at me perplexed. The other Viewers came around and noticed I had the appearance of physical burn marks on my face and arms, which disappeared about 15 minutes later. I was immediately given the disclosure for this session and it was the firebombing of Dresden during WWII.

I was pretty shaken by this and didn't understand it. How and why did this happen? I had gotten pretty good at remote viewing, but having an extreme visceral experience and reaction such as this had not occurred before, and it took on a whole new level for me. I asked Pru and others why this would happen and the response was "perhaps you had a past life there?" I wasn't convinced. In the back of my mind, this intense experience seemed to coincide with the action of using my whole body within a session, but I still felt confused by it all. The glaringly obvious though, was that a Remote Viewer is not a disinterested and disconnected anthropologist taking notes. You can be fully immersed and take part in something occurring in the past, or even in the future. There is another question as well... how do we, as Remote Viewers, affect the remote location or event that we become part of? I didn't have time for these questions at the moment because the class was moving forward quickly, so I pushed it back and kept going.

Occasionally interrupting this class were some perplexing situations. One of the events was a silent triangular craft probably 100 feet off the ground hovering over the house, and emitting a very loud and directional trumpet sound in the night time after the class had ended one day. For the two people who saw this, it sent them into complete panic and fear. This was explained by Pru afterward as a warning that we are not to remote view any classified information. Unknown to us Viewers, we had in fact been tasked on something classified the previous day. The first flight of the stealth bomber. It was not classified at the moment we had the class, nor the moment we viewed it, but the first flight and the military base where it occurred was - Area 51.

Another curious event was that Pru's house had been viciously vandalized a day or two before the class started. Smashed up inside and out, unknown vandals spray painted on the garage door expletives and death threats. This was explained by her as typical harassment she'd been experiencing of late. She even pulled out a small microphone looking object which she claimed to have found behind an outlet cover - an eavesdropping device. To me it could have been anything, kids messing around, an overactive imagination... I was withholding judgment overall, but you did hear about other bits of intrigue within the remote viewing community, especially when you stepped outside of the "ex"-military circles. Even though I held back on judgment, I did begin to cast a suspicious eye, and wonder if anyone in this particular class was a spook.

The whole idea of this particular class was to form a group which could become the core of a working remote viewing think tank. While some people trained would fade into obscurity - like the person who wanted to have "remote viewing uniforms" for everyone, or the one who spoke loudly about how crystals placed on his penis was an exhilarating moment for him. But one of the scariest incidents occurred when one person nearly died from a bleeding ulcer during the class. He claimed he was being remote influenced, and it could be coming from someone who was taking that very class. He ended up in the hospital nearly dead from it. Regardless of who was sticking around or not, there was a lot of talk about how we could make money, and treasure hunting was one of those ways.

I was to be a Viewer on this session so I didn't know what I was to view, nor did I know it was treasure related. I only knew I needed to cool down and then meet up with my monitor.

Cooling down is a process a Remote Viewer goes through before a session in order to subdue the thinking mind, and drop into a meditative state. We will typically listen to binaural beats during this period which accelerates the meditative state. Ultimately, we want to reach a deep alpha state where we can dip in and out of theta.

Think of an EKG here, a line with peaks and valleys. The normal awake and thought filled mind exists in a beta state which has high peaks and valleys, and a lot of them. As you slow the thoughts down and disconnect, you begin to drift into alpha where the peaks and valleys start to spread out a bit -- a meditative state. Theta exists just beyond alpha and is the precursor to delta, or sleep. A Remote Viewer wants to get into theta as much as possible in order to grab visuals, bi-locate, and get generally good information on an objective. It also has the ability to suspend memories and allow a flow to occur where you don't get so caught up in trying to figure out what you're remote viewing. You do not necessarily need to manipulate your mind state in order to remote view, but this can help to clear some of the thoughts away.

Theta is in the realm of 4 to 7 hertz, so a

binaural beat which has the potential to drag you there, would work by pumping in one ear a sound at 6 hertz, and in another ear, a sound at 4 hertz. The brain will then synchronize to 5 hertz, and you will begin to feel relaxed as you disconnect from your thoughts and drift away.

My monitor went off to another location to cool down a bit and grab some AP's (advanced perceptuals - images and sensations written down on a piece of paper during a cool down process which often relate to the objective). My monitor was blind to the objective, as was I, and was instructed to give me movement exercises at certain points in the session.

I began my cool down, pumping theta sounds into my brain, when I found myself within a scene. My feet were on warm golden sand, and I was enjoying the feeling of this heat as I pushed each toe deep into it. Just beyond my feet I saw a beautiful azure blue pool of shallow water within what appeared to be a desert alcove made of sandstone.

Suddenly a hairy, small, and excited creature of some sort, jumped into this scene from the side of the alcove. He zipped around flailing his arms and legs in partial dance moves and partial attention grabbing. As he danced, in a stilted sing-songy voice he said, "connect with me during your next session and I will help you!" I opened my eyes, rubbed them a bit and thought to myself, "I am making up some crazy shit".

My monitor and I were given the creepy dark garage to do our session, while the other Remote Viewers got the comfort of a warm house. The sun was beginning to go down and we made our way to the card table where there was little light, except for a lonely bulb swinging back and forth, casting swaying shadows in every spider filled corner. A place you couldn't help but imagine that someone may have hung themselves there in a time past, or ran their car with the garage door closed until it filled with carbon monoxide.

My monitor and I sat down and he had me begin the session. The first page, what we call scan 1, was uneventful. Rocks, dirt, some concrete foundations, just mundane descriptions... The second page, scan two, started to get a bit interesting. In that scan I perceived a subject, which can be any type of being, physical or non-physical. This particular subject was short and had hair all over its body, like a mini-Bigfoot. The face of the subject was covered with hair and it exuded a trickster vibe.

I was not able to relate this particular subject to my previous vision, because when you remote view, and do so from the standpoint of deep alpha and theta, your memory does not work in a normal linear fashion. I had also shoved that event away at the time, mostly chalking it up to an overactive imagination.

As I was working on describing this

subject, all at once I understood it was a paraphysical being (a subject existing outside of 3D reality) and completely aware of me.

I began to feel a hot and cold tingling sensation covering my right shoulder, and as I began to write out this sensation, its invisible hand grabbed me hard and held on tight. I refrained from jumping out of the chair, bolting into the relative safety of the house, and instead I looked up, and calmly told my monitor... "Ok, this subject is grabbing my shoulder". My monitor looks at me with a bit of fear in his eyes, and so I ask him what he wants me to do. He tells me to drop my pen and maybe it will go away! Within remote viewing we often drop our pen when we want to signal to our brain to let go and move on from specific data we get, and it was slightly comical hearing this in regard to being harassed by a paraphysical, but hey, he was thinking on his feet. I was also more than willing to try anything in order to get it off of me.

After a minute or so it relented and I moved on with the session, when suddenly, I began to see the shadow of this creature moving in the garage, dive bombing us. As I continued on, trying to write down impressions, I began ducking this way and that to avoid the shadow. Then it happened again - I started to feel the hot and tingly sensation on my leg just before it grabbed me, and at the same time, I got another brief glimpse of the subject's hairy face.

My monitor was completely freaked, visibly shaking, with fear in his voice, while he guided me through the rest of the session. Even though we felt attacked by the paraphysical activity occurring in a creepy dark garage, we were stalwart in getting through the session in full.

By this time I realized the being was the one from my vision while I was cooling down just a half hour ago, and in between the grabbing and dive bombing, I was receiving data which was clearly treasure related. The assault was relentless and there was no way I was going to connect with him as he suggested!

When we finished the session, the sun was completely down and pitch black, save for a small bulb and spiders hanging over us. My monitor looks at me with dread in his eyes, and in a slow and shaky manner he pulls out a piece of paper, holding it trembling in front of me. This was a sketch he did before we did the session, and was part of his AP's (advanced perceptuals). It was a sketch of the hairy faced trickster.

At that moment, the communication occurring between us was only an agreement between our eyes; no words. We stayed strong, and completed our task. In the face of adversity we kept our wits about us. Now though, we run. And we did.

Both of us smashing though the garage door at the same time, shoulder to shoulder, we came upon an excited scene in the house. The other Viewers had finished sessions on the same thing, and all of them were approached by the same hairy faced being. This being also wanted them to connect with him, which they did, and all the data was completely confused and different. There was nothing at all to corroborate between sessions in order to get a better understanding.

This was the Lost Dutchman's Treasure, and it was clear it was being protected by a strong paraphysical, which amounts to the dreaded treasure curse. A clear no-go.

More importantly though, I realized the very fine line between what we think we create in our heads, and something else trying to communicate with us. You know those errant images and faces that float through your mind's eye, or random thoughts popping into your head? Is it you, or something else? Believe me, not all of it is you.

Another thing that hit home - beings who exist outside of our 3D reality, paraphysicals, will know when you remote view them and will interact with you. From ghosts, to extradimensionals, to ET's. If you have one of those within a session you can be sure they will let you know they are there, sometimes even paying you a visit after the session.

A bond forms with people during these two week classes. Consciousness begins to meld into a cohesive group mind as a deeper psychic energy ramps up and takes hold. You can feel the singular and shared energy moving through the group, and it seems to build more trust between people, but you can't blindly trust that trust.

With a crew cut and his accent, you would think he was in the SAS and the British government sent him to our class for some training. I knew that's what most others were thinking, but intuitively I could tell it wasn't the case. Intense, tough, and a fighter, he and I formed a quick bond for some reason. He also had a unique knack for naming exactly what the objective was, and getting it correct. You could sense an incongruence in his demeanor, up against what we were doing, which was why there was distrust, but the reality of "why", became apparent as the class progressed.

The incongruent sense we all felt was shown to be the conflict he had with what he was doing here. A large part of his current mental construct would not accept the reality of what he could do, and a massive bleeding ulcer developed during the class due to his conflict.

It can be the case, where extreme physical manifestations occur when metal conflicts arise like this. Blaming it on a psychic attack, rather than his own mind, he ended up in the hospital for days, because it nearly killed him.

In Pru's backyard there were a number of people camping for the two weeks, and one was a couple from the Midwest. I can imagine the neighbors were thinking we were some sort of strange cult. Here is a woman whose house is vandalized with death threats for all to see, then she has 15 people coming and going for two weeks, with some camping in her backyard. Suburbia thrives on lockstep normalcy and the location she lived in was very cookie-cutter. When I came and went my stomach always tightened up as the neighbors watched me with damnation in their eyes.

I've lived on both coasts, New York and California, but I haven't spent any time in the Midwest. Based on my experiences with Midwesterners, I imagine a land full of (mostly) grounded, steady, kind and deeply moralistic people. That's been my experience making friends with them while living on the coasts, but I apologize for being a little naive.

It was no different with this Midwestern couple. You set aside any pretenses and just connect, as it's almost what is demanded. Suspecting they were anything but a nice couple from the Midwest would be heresy. Making quick friends, we would hang out together during the breaks, scheming and concocting a remote viewing plan for after the class was over.

At times I felt like a drooling space cadet zoning out in the ethers, and it was because I was constantly pumping theta sounds into my brain. I also knew this was what was making me so damn good. With every objective, I was dropping in and getting amazing visuals, as well as good data consistently. So I embarked on the last session for this class with that as my wind.

It was a remarkably unremarkable session while I was doing it, only because of an expectation I would be viewing some crazy UFO related paranormal treasure hunting blowout. None of that was there.

My perceptions centered around a man who was being somewhat sketchy and nefarious. He was surreptitiously recording things, sending that information off to someone and then getting notes back on more things to do. Within the context of past sessions, it was somewhat boring visually, so I decided I needed to really dig in and grab some images. Maybe I'll see something cool and paranormal like an alien or UFO!

We did have a monitor on this session and mine was my new friend from the Midwest guiding me through, asking me questions, and pushing me to dig as deep as I could.

I readied myself and closed my eyes to pop a visual or two, maybe even bi-locate. You never know. I relaxed and dropped down into another clear visual. I see a man in a long black trench coat with dark hair using a device to communicate with others because he was on some type of lone assignment. Then, like a flash, I was looking right at his face in a close-up, and wouldn't you know it, it's the guy sitting across from me, my monitor and new friend!

Why? I thought quickly because there was a lot of strange stuff going on in the session and it made me uncomfortable, but I had to deduct him, and so I did. I said aloud, "why do I see you? I see a clear image of you." He didn't say anything, but looked at me oddly, so I just placed it in the deduction[1] column and moved on with the session.

The thing is, I couldn't ignore it; I had found that when a visual comes from that deep hypnagogic state, it is usually correct. It wasn't like it was general sensory impressions coming through. I knew whatever I was viewing had to do with him somehow.

We tied up the session and I was excited to hear what we just viewed. I got the piece of paper with the disclosure and opened it up: "Describe the individual or individuals closest to

---

[1] A deduction in Remote Viewing is a high level conclusion. If I were to come to a conclusion during a session on what I am remote viewing, as opposed to just describing what is occurring, I would place this bit of information off to the side and go back to just describing at a low level. An example would be - within an RV session I am getting a lot of impressions of people fighting, destruction, water, explosions and I decide to say it is The Pearl Harbor Attack. The naming of Pearl Harbor Attack is a deduction.

our current location from the team conducting the harassment and interested in our activities."

I thought, if you can't trust the trustworthy, then who can you trust?

CHAPTER SEVEN
The Treasure Set-Up

With a regular cue of sessions given to us after the two week class, we were all motivated to get something substantial going. There was a feeling we were on the cusp of something big.

Word came from another prominent Remote Viewer that a Treasure Hunter he knew needed a bit of assistance. Apparently this Treasure Hunter made some finds in the past but was stuck on a project he was working on in the Arizona desert. The other Remote Viewer was too busy with other projects, so it was sent our way. We would get a cut of whatever we could find, and he would get a finder's fee.

Being a primary Remote Viewer, I had to remain blind to the project, so I didn't know at first, other than we had a job coming. I was working a cue of five remote viewing sessions per week and these just dropped into my workload, so for me it was business as usual. Sometimes they were monitored sessions over the phone or in person, and sometimes they were solo. In total, there were five of us remote viewing on this project.

A couple of sessions in, it becomes easy to identify what you're working on. Flashes of crosses and jewels along with a desert environment and you get it. I also knew whatever we were going after was a big load and worth a lot just by the volume and age of the items I was picking up on in the sessions.

Something wasn't right though. In between the sessions, within the noise of my normal life, I began to notice something that was never there before. A sketchy van began to park regularly right outside my house and a white pickup truck liked to follow me around on occasion. Add to that, odd clicking noises and static pervading the land-line on monitored sessions, I became a bit paranoid someone was interested in this project.

Taking small bits of information, the thinking mind comes to a shaky conclusion on what is occurring. While I battled with the thought of being overly paranoid, my body was telling me something different.

I have done quite a bit of martial arts in

my life, and when I was a kid I spent years within Tang Soo Do Karate. During my time in training, the teacher would sometimes line us kids up with our face to a wall and our backs to him. With a tennis ball in his hand he would choose a kid, raise his hand, and mentally focus just before he let it loose. Because we could not see him, we had to learn to rely on a sixth sense to indicate we were about to get beaned in the back of the head with a ball. If his target did not raise a hand, that person would get hit.

When he first did this, every kid would scrunch up and raise a hand so they wouldn't get hit, me included. As we kept practicing, I began to notice a feeling in my body when he was about to throw it at me. It was like an indefinable point of focus, or pressure on my back, and when I felt that, I would raise my hand.

On this occasion my body was feeling the same. Someone was really focused in on me and the project, no matter what my brain was telling me. From this, I found I could know the truth of nearly anything by allowing my body and "gut" to feel it first before sending it into my brain.

Over a couple of months we worked through many sessions on the treasure. From the reality of it, to the retrieval method, nothing was left out and it resulted in hundreds of pages of data. The last session of the project was particularly interesting, which was to be a monitored session over the phone.

The usual clicks, static and pops occurred, but I was too far gone to really care. I had spent my waking moment until the session time listening to binaural beats and meditating. When my monitor finally called, I had trouble even figuring out how to answer the phone. Once he said his greeting to me, I remarked, "you how are John, good?" I couldn't even remember his name, so I garbled it up and called him me. His response was, "Oooookkkk, that's a good sign, let's get started!"

This strange dyslexia would also occur when I was going for my fine art degree. Out of nowhere I would begin writing and speaking backwards after working on a painting for a couple of hours, and it took some effort to reverse it. I also had a condition called Alice in Wonderland Syndrome which would create incredible spatial distortions where I would feel extremely tiny or gigantic within my surroundings. Add the two together and occurring at the same time, which it sometimes would, and interactions had the potential to go haywire. Trying to speak to someone 500 feet away from me, my speech backwards, or just sweating it out hoping I wouldn't do anything crazy.

I raced into that session full of visuals and very clear impressions. Treasures are meant to be hidden, which means the locations are usually non-descript and unassuming, making it difficult to locate it on the ground, even though the

Viewers can bring you great descriptions. The nice thing about this one, was I perceived that it was not buried, and the final resting place was very unique from the overall surroundings. I felt, at least from my own session data, I could find the location easily.

You'll often find with treasures that a spirit is hanging around and protecting them, and they do come forward during remote viewing sessions. A very important aspect is to determine if this spirit is going to try and lead you into danger, or mislead you -- the dreaded treasure curse like we ran into when we worked the Lost Dutchman.

This project had a particular spirit who was an old cowboy hovering around it protectively. He had been involved in collecting the goods and placing them here, but like many treasures that still lay hidden, he was killed before he could get back to it, which created a huge attachment to it. The treasure itself was crosses, jewelry, swords, gold coins and bars all stolen from a Mission, and worth a substantial amount of money at the time he took it.

At first the cowboy was hanging on the edges just watching me, and when it came time during the session, I had to approach him. Up to that moment in my remote viewing life, I had come across many paraphysicals, which I would typically interact with a bit, get the info I needed, and then move on. Something strange happened this time, and it was all to do with a request my monitor made. He asked me if I would like to blend with this cowboy, which means I would become him and would feel as though I were him. When you do a blend within a session, it has the consequence of shifting your consciousness to the point of feeling how they feel as opposed to describing how they feel. Problem was, this was a damn ghost! Blending with dead humans is typically not the best thing to do.

I thought about it for about a second, and said "what the hell, let's go".

Strange smells and desires of whiskey and tobacco consumed me while I began to speak to my monitor in a western drawl. I could see his life as if it were mine and the circumstances of his death; shot in the chest and gut multiple times. A cagey cowboy with humor, wit and give a fuck attitude. My monitor asked him many questions, many of which I can't recall because my consciousness seemed to blink further and further away the longer he was in. I do remember one thing he said. In order for us to retrieve anything without his interference, he wanted to have another Remote Viewer on the team, a female, do a session and connect with him, because he had the hots for her. If we could do that, he claimed he would even help out how he could. Poor girl has to take one for the team, and I didn't envy her.

Once I came back from this, I was a hot mess. Dyslexic from all the binaural beats, on top of a dead drunk cowboy being in me, I was feeling a little weird. But before completely ending, my monitor wanted one more thing.

"I want you to do a movement exercise. I want you to shift to the person outside of our team who is most interested in this project at this very moment". This request was made because I was completely in the zone and my data excellent. Also, from the perspective of everyone on the team, we were closely monitored at the moment through electronic and other physical means.

Immediately upon hearing his request, and without doing a thing, I saw a van on a suburban street. I recognized the neighborhood, and I recognized my monitor's house within this neighborhood. About a block from his location there was a van, which had the markings on it of utility service, but it was a fake. Inside was a subject seated at a desk with a panel of knobs and switches. He was intercepting our communications by running through the local phone line, connected as he was through a utility box.

I created what we call a Consciousness Map of this subject and began to grab everything I could from his mind. I began to watch him in real time, and as I described him in physical detail along with what he was doing and thinking, he began to get very uncomfortable. I could feel and see his frustration and anxiety mount to the point where he snapped a pencil in half, jumped in the driver's seat and prepared to take off. At that moment we knew we were being watched and my monitor cut the call fast so he could go out and catch a glimpse. On the other side of that, there was nothing we could do about it except watch our backs, but I think we had already missed the boat on that one.

The big question is, who are these people? They were obviously very sophisticated in their eavesdropping. Could the Treasure Hunter we were working with have hired a team of people to steal our data, or perhaps it's a rival Treasure Hunter? We had our assumptions but we didn't really talk about them except in quiet whispers, nor did we discuss any of it in email or over the phone for fear we would reveal what we knew to them.

The time came then to head to the treasure site in Arizona, connect with the Treasure Hunter, and get the lay of the land. The data was clear and the path was set, so it seemed a fairly easy find. I was not to head out to the location, as my job was to hang back at home, stay in communication and remote view on the fly if needed, while Pru and an analyst on the project headed out to investigate. If it took more than a couple of days, then I was to head out and help.

They arrived after about a five hour drive, then settled in at their hotel before making their way out to meet up with the Treasure Hunter. We had our report, but more things shake loose when you get to the site and investigate. Lining elements up can be both easy and frustrating, but for this one it seems an easy find because the treasure is not buried, rather, it's dropped in between some cracks in a rock.

They met him before sunset to get it going as fast as possible, and hopefully recover it that day... it's not like you had to spend any time digging it up.

When they parked and met up with the Treasure Hunter he began to guide them into the location, but there was a slight issue - they were walking into a national monument. Assuming they were to just pass through the monument outside of its boundaries, there were no real concerns as they walked.

When you work with a Treasure Hunter, they won't tell you the location beforehand in order to keep it secret, in case you get some funny ideas. Quickly, the situation went from questionable to downright illegal. Within the boundaries of this federally protected land they came upon numerous large holes he had been digging in search of this treasure! Any "successful" and "long time" Treasure Hunter knows you cannot, and must not dig within a national monument, as it's a federal crime amounting to a felony; jail-time is pretty much a guarantee.

At that point he was questioned about this, and Pru told him we would have absolutely nothing to do with it, and if we had known it was on protected land an agreement would never have been made. Arguing ensued and he was trying to coerce the data out of her. To make it all worse, the analyst from our team began to argue on the side of the Treasure Hunter. In fact the analyst said they should go back when it gets dark, jump the fence and retrieve it, which the Treasure Hunter heartily agreed with!

The curious thing here is, we know virtually nothing about this Treasure Hunter, we had not met him before this, and one of our team members is arguing to conduct an illegal act knowing full well that we are also being watched closely. Our team member even went so far as to verbally assault Pru's character for not agreeing to this.

Pru stayed steady in her conviction that it wasn't going to happen and asked that she be taken back to the hotel. She would find her way back home and not ride back with him.

I received a call from Pru after this was over, the next day, and she relayed the story. As we were talking she had to take another call. When she got back to me, she said it was the FBI calling her, and we have to go into their field office in San Diego because they got a tip we were digging in a National Monument. So they received a tip we were digging in a national monument around midnight or so? Not that there was any digging going on by our group, but how would they know this fast we were even there and who we are? The time spent at the site was likely around two hours.

From the Remote Viewer who sent it our way, to the Treasure Hunter, to one of our own people, we had been set up. If the route had been taken of jumping the fence and going after it, federal agents would have swarmed in at that moment, and it would have been all over.

It was 100% clear we were a threat to someone and had to be done away with, but why? Remote viewing is declassified and there should be no issue.

John Vivanco

CHAPTER EIGHT
Root of Creativity

Up to the point before I eventually headed off to college, around age 22, my world had been playing in bands, with all my thoughts and desires revolving around getting signed to a record label. We even had a manger who was hustling gigs, and trying to get us signed. We were just a three piece; I played bass and lead vocals, and we were part of the early Emo scene in Encinitas, California. Emo stands for "emotive", or "emotional", and it's kind of a melodic post-punk grunge with impassioned singing and lyrics.

We were becoming popular, until our drummer got into a drunk driving accident and nearly killed a good friend who was the passenger, placing him in jail for eight months. Between the three of us there was a creative tension working perfectly in its tumultuousness, but when he got out, there was only tumultuousness. He was a sensitive person and so the guilt really got to him. He ended up self-medicating constantly, and it increasingly got more extreme until it was just heroin.

Inevitably the band broke up, so I jumped around playing with others, but it was never the same, and it was the only plan I had. I was committed to the idea of a band life, but it felt like that dream was done, and I had to figure out a new path. My best friend from the band, the guitarist, headed off to art school so I decided I would follow. It seemed like a good idea to get a Bachelor of Fine Art and most importantly, postpone things for four years.

I wasn't one who grew up drawing or painting, which you typically find in art school, nor did I have a passion for it. My interest lay more in understanding the root of creativity and from there, to know what life is, and who I am. I wanted to know what it meant to be creative and what happens when you live completely in it, within every moment. The band life showed me a bit of that, but it wasn't enough to take me anywhere meaningful, and it felt important to do it completely alone, as opposed to within a group.

Often in my life, the ideas I have about what I want don't go the way of my mental calculations. It's as though there's a driving force under the surface of my conscious life, which seems to know the better path, and sometimes I have to give into it, even though it's a struggle. If my life were a tree, the idea I had of the band life would be a branch of the tree, in the direction I want to grow. The thing is, if those branches don't serve the overall growth of the tree, they will die. They grow for the benefit of the whole tree and don't often align with a desire, even though there is an aspect of what the whole tree wants wrapped up in the desire. I fought that notion hard, because I wanted so badly for the band to come into full fruition.

From creating in a band to creating in an art school, the art school branch is not that different than the band branch on the surface - but it is very different underneath. It likely won't kill me.

When I was in art school I was reading books from thinkers like RD Laing and other fringe writers. They believed madness, for the most part, was light cracking through the surface of a mind trying to deal with the contradictions of life and society, up against what true reality is. The contradictions being what we are told vs. a mind becoming illumined, and the individual not being able to deal with it mentally, which causes some kind of break.

I was interested in the line between realization and insanity, pure creative genius, and primarily where that line of interpretation was. Most of all, the path to get there. Often times there seemed no difference between a societally judged insane person, and a realized person. I wanted to push myself to that edge and see if I could experience and understand this root where creativity meets with madness and truth. I suppose it's that thin line a lot of artists seem to skirt.

It wasn't so much about the artwork I produced, as it was more the process and the drive to be completely within the creative source at all times. To become the root as opposed to producing blindly from that root. I was studying and writing papers on the relationship between creative genius, enlightenment and madness when I wasn't producing artwork. I wasn't by any means mad, but I could at times begin to feel a line into pure creativity that walked the edge of madness – like balancing on a mental knife point. At one one moment, I felt as though all the Universe would become known, but in the next, it would frustratingly disappear.

Consumed with this process, I had also been religiously meditating and going to a Zen Center on a regular basis. The center, being in San Diego County, and I was in Orange County, meant a lot of driving, so I couldn't go as often as I liked. The silence is deafening at the Zen Center, and it was a respite from the chaos in my head, so as much as I could, I would scrape my gas change together and make it.

I had come down with the flu and missed going for a couple of weeks, and I was too weak and tired to meditate at home. I had to head down to the center, and wanted to meditate at least a little before that, so I sat on my cushion and tried. About 15 minutes into a half-hour meditation session I began to feel... not right. Some type of information was hitting my brain, and my brain could not deal with it, but oddly, I didn't know what that information was. The breathing down into my stomach began to get shallower and move higher in my chest, so I stopped. I figured it must be because I was getting over the flu.

At the Zen Center the next day I took my space in the Zendo (meditation hall) on my cushion, as the first of a handful of 30 minute sessions began. It was the same as before, 10 to 15 minutes into it, the feeling came back, but this time it was much more intense, and the "information" (f you can call it that) was like a freight train slamming into a wall.

There were spaces and distances, but no spaces and distances. I could feel myself as the person next to me, but still I was me, in my body. I could feel the building as me, yet I am also in my body. I was everything at once, but to the brain it was clearly not correct. It was such an extreme, expansive, visceral and ongoing experience, as opposed to a brief glimpse, that I started to hyperventilate and panic. It was the kind of experience I was looking for, but it was all a horrifying ongoing and intense contradiction to a self-identity, and a big part of me wasn't having any of it. In fact, it felt as though my brain was actually heating up trying to process, or bury it, in order to control the situation.

At that point I succumbed to panic. I doubled over on my cushion as I began to hyperventilate, when the people sitting next to me noticed, and ushered me out of the meditation hall and into a little side office. It then took an unexpected turn.

Here are people who are well versed in the experiential pitfalls and high points of going inside yourself. A bunch of ex-hippies who have probably talked a lot of people out of bad trips, and if I just tried to explain to them what was happening, they would have been able to help me. Instead, I played it up as though I was still sick with the flu, because I was 99.9% convinced (irrationally) that they were going to put me in an insane asylum. Somehow, I was convinced. The contradictions lessened a bit and moved to the background while this paranoid notion completely took over. It was very difficult for me to act "normal", but I knew I had to convince them I was sane and good to go. I felt trapped within the tiny office we were in, laughing nervously and in complete panic internally, because I was beginning to think I was a paranoid schizophrenic, and they knew it as well.

When I finally left, my hour drive was full of panic attacks, and part of it was because I was utterly convinced they had called an asylum or facility to come and get me. Within the depths of my panic, I felt an intense and visceral mental contradiction of everything. It wasn't like anything I had ever felt before. Of course there were moments when I felt "one" with everything, or had a deeper realization of it within tiny increments, but this was like buying the coat as opposed to just trying it on.

RD Laing had said: "Creative people who can't help but explore other mental territories are at greater risk, just as someone who climbs a mountain is more at risk than someone who just walks along a village lane."

As I got home, the intensity subsided, but I could see shadows seemingly in wait. Finally being able to drift into some form of unconsciousness, I straddled a realm between full sleep and awake. I slipped into another one of those visions of past lives which seem to follow me.

I saw a man in 18th Century Britain. He was old with a long beard, and had been locked up in an asylum for a long period of time. A dank, dark atmosphere with thick brick walls, he spent his time looking through a window that afforded a small view of the sky. He would mumble to himself about how he was the spider crawling on the wall, or the cloud that moved past his window.

More than anything, he didn't want to be in this place, but his family had placed him here because of crazy talk and paranoia. His brain had fractured with the contradictions perceived in the outside world and what he was taught, up against his experience of what reality truly is. He was unable to deal with the immensity and beauty of truth, that is the oneness of everything, and he was a rambling wreck with no one to help guide him. It was too much to realize for a brain that was not ready, like something soft being tossed into a bag full of razor blades. As much in the light of pure beauty, as he was in the darkness of an unaccepting and cracked mind.

As I watched, I knew he was me, and when I realized this, I heard a voice behind me. The voice told me that the fracture currently happening is what needs to occur in order to clean it up; to take another step forward. "Be with it, meditate with it, do not react to it, it will gradually dissipate and you will enter into a new phase. Know that it is not you in this life creating it. It is something which needs to be cleaned up energetically, and you are now in place to do it."

In the days following, it happened frequently, but as the voice said it would dissipate, so it did. The pushing and pulling of a sensation of being another and myself at the same time, or being everywhere at once, hit the wall of construct that was collapsing. Light cracking through the surface.

Once it settled, I felt as though I became the creative source, the root. There was no tapping into it, no pulling on it in order to draw it in, no waiting for a muse. It was I always, and within any situation. There was also a more integrated and mellow sense of feeling connected with everything, and not an overwhelming visceral event.

At this point, producing art meant very little, and I could take it or leave it. Creativity is the constantly unfolding life, not locked up in a painting or a piece of music. It's the nature of the moment.

There's a Zen story where a master wakes up one of his students at 2am to take him somewhere special. As the master takes the groggy monk on this hike they soon hit a hill. For hours they climb in the pitch blackness, the monk struggling upward and falling down because of the steepness and the loose rocks. Barely able to go any further they finally reach the top just as the sun was cresting the curvature of the earth and illuminating where they were. The monk asks, where are we? The master says look around. As the monk viewed his surroundings, he was standing on the top of a mountain, but the mountain was made completely of skulls and bones, in fact as far as he could see it was skulls and bones. The monk cries, "where have you taken me"! The master says, "these are all of your past lives".

I have a lot to clean up if that's the case, or I should say, let go of. Each one of those lives is cause and effect, spinning and transferring more and more to each life, unless you are somehow unraveling it.

All the attachments we've created over all the lives we've lived, creates an energy in need of resolution, or letting go of. Very strong emotions create an energy and attachment to things which keep cause and effect moving, otherwise known as Karma. It is often that the very intense situations occurring in our lives is the energy from the deep past making its rounds. Sometimes you have no idea where it came from, and you hit back at it with intense emotion and perplexity, which causes that wheel of suffering to keep spinning. Just the act of paying attention to what was occurring inside of me brought me out on the other side of this, and released the energy of it. It was a place of allowing it to move through me without reacting to it with emotions and creating stories around it.

CHAPTER NINE
The Start Up

"We got an investor!" When word came I was very excited. For one, a core of us would receive a salary to remote view full time. Another - I am an introvert with a bit of agoraphobia on the edges, so my next thought was - I don't have to go outside anymore, I can just watch the world unfold from inside my mind!

I had been working freelance, developing concepts for Wet Seal and Contempo stores, and then Urban Outfitters, but it was a grind and typically under contract. In other words, it always ended. I never gave thought to remote viewing being something I would do full time, so it was somewhat of a surprise, and something I wouldn't think twice about doing.

It was a relatively quick set up, TDS

(Trans Dimensional Systems) was formed and off we went. At that point there were four of us working for the company and we primarily remote viewed. Two people were in Hawaii, while Pru and I were in Southern California. Our cue was two to three sessions per day, five days a week. Each session could sometimes run two hours long, but most were just over an hour. Because of the cool down period I would do before sessions, I was in a meditative state all day, day after day.

At a certain point you become what feels like a singular and exposed clairvoyant nerve cell. There was talk in the remote viewing world, primarily coming from the ex-military circles, that remote viewing this amount over a period of time can make you go insane. They call it "destabilization".

A different matter altogether is the increase in empathy, and it was reminiscent of my early childhood where I shut down because of the intensity. If I wasn't careful, I could get sucked into an ever expanding fractal of introversion with this. To me it goes without saying, but if you do this in a full-time capacity, you have to ground yourself and stay in a physical reality. It may be that those in the military program don't, or didn't give much thought to it, and they have no techniques to help people deal with it - hence their idea of destabilization. If you're already destabilized to begin with, and never seek being stable, how can you expect to remain stable while doing this?

Many CEO's out there had already heard of remote viewing, especially those in the technology sector. If they hadn't heard of it before the Sony news article came out, they would then. The news article came from an internal leak at Sony which referred to a team of Remote Viewers on staff for their product development. Interestingly, Sony didn't deny it, but they did say they no longer *cough* use them.

Because of that article, as well as the contacts our investor had, we both contacted and were approached by many CEO's across many business sectors. I know this is a generalization, but the mind of a successful CEO is often quite different than the average person. In other words, as a population we are given information with a conclusion built in, for instance, in news reports. It's also often that the conclusion is geared to direct overall thought in a specific direction, whether it's true or not. For the most part, I found many company heads don't work with pre-configured information packets and conclusions built in like most of the population. They come to their own conclusions based on many data points from varied sources, and often do not care what the source of information is, as long as it's reliable.

For us, there is no one else in the company we can speak to. It has to be the person making big decisions and is free to take from any source they want. Nonetheless, we still had to go through the back door because of the controversial nature of what we do.

We had a technology transfer protocol, which is slightly different than the normal remote viewing protocol, and was a huge point of interest for product development in certain companies. If you could remote view the future, bringing back patentable ideas, you could have a serious leg up on your competitors.

Imagine though, you are a person living in the 10th century, and have a vision you know is from the future. You find yourself in the year 2016 at Heathrow Airport, watching a jumbo jet take off and fly into the air. When you get back to your time, how do you explain this to someone? You can give a description of what occurred based on the context of your time. "It was an iron eagle larger than a house, with fire and smoke shooting out of its back!" Of course it is a correct and contextually related description, but that doesn't really describe what it is and what it does. Would they understand the mechanics, parts and functioning of a jet engine, and all the controls that go into it, much less describe that? It would be like magic to them. That is the conundrum you're faced with when you dig into future technologies.

A curiosity was always there with these executives that I found humorous. We would talk business, give them data on real world problems and solutions, then after that, most would start to feel around with "alien" type questions. It so happens, once they see useful data, they want to hear about the projects we work with more of an off-planet bent. The rest of the day would inevitably be a drawn out Oprah type interview on aliens and esoterica we encountered.

As we were setting up meetings with CEO's and others, there would be excitement and interest in exploring the possibilities, but just before the meeting time, they would cancel, never to be heard from again. Even though some got through, we got word most were being warned off by a faceless entity, but there was no way to know who, because they kept quiet about it as they quickly slipped out of communication.

Pru and I would typically meet at the beach and other public places in order to talk sensitive business issues and security. It was already demonstrated many times - we had become a target. I was working projects in order to figure out the who's and the whys of it all because I took on the overall responsibility of security, which is kind of a laugh. I probably went from a blubbery, soft target, to just a soft target.

Our overall intentions were very clear and clean. We would never use RV for illegal purposes, corporate espionage, hurting people or violence in anyway, etc... We are compassionate people who want the highest good for the world we live in and the people we come in contact with. I was fully involved with Buddhism and the compassion developed from that, while Pru was also practicing compassion in action and Buddhist meditation herself. Ultimately it was confusing, because I was thrust into this world in an unexpected way. I had to figure out who they were and how we could stop this.

I had no idea about counter-espionage, other than what I saw in the movies, so I had to learn fast. Meet-ups in public places with lots of noise, remove battery from cell phone (when you could), check car for tracking devices (unless you have "OnStar", then you're really screwed), drive in unpredictable ways to make sure you're not being followed... It really didn't matter though, because I was the only one doing it and there were way too many holes to cover! I'm sure they were laughing at my attempts to slip past them.

At a certain point you could always tell they were there, but it's after the fact and somewhat of a moot point. At least at the beach, there was the potential they could not hear us over crashing waves, or so we thought.

On one occasion Pru and I ended up at a jetty, with the loudest crashing beach waves we knew, so we could have some conversations around death threats we had received - who was doing it, and what projects we were working on.

While we were sitting on the sand, a squirrel was running in and out of the rocks that comprise the jetty, getting as close to us as possible. We were laughing and discussing the possibility it was a remote control squirrel with a listening device on it, because of how it was acting.

After a couple of minutes of this, two people approached us from the rear. One looked homeless with a scruffy beard and dirty white clothes. The other had greasy black hair pressed down into a line of bangs on his forehead, in somewhat of a bowl cut. His tight green polyester pants were too short, like he was waiting for a flood, and his green Hawaiian shirt was an abomination. He looked like he had just gotten off a bus from somewhere in the Midwest where there were absolutely no fashion rules. They stood next to us trying to talk about the squirrel, laughing and yelling that it looked like a little robot squirrel.

Something was not right, and our senses heightened. The two men pulled back, wandered in the background shouting about robot squirrels, and along comes an African American male wearing your typical California casual clothes. Completely unassuming, with the appearance of a guy from an office on his lunch break, he was walking normally with arms swinging as they typically do when someone walks. As we watched, we noticed he had a disposable camera in one hand, yet held in a way where the lens was pointing at us. As he walked and swung his arms, he deftly operated the camera. With a single thumb he would click a photo as he walked past us, and then wind it with that single thumb. He repeated the process in a slow stroll as he went past, keeping the lens trained on us. He made his way to the end of the jetty, playing it up as if he were contemplating the beautiful scenery, then walked by us again with the same clicking and winding.

Behind us was a parked RV, and as he disappeared from view on the other side, I decided to run and peer around the corner to see where he was going. When I got around the RV, the robot squirrel men were right there with him. He handed the camera to the green pants spook, shook his hand, and when they saw me they took off in different directions. Looking down the beach I spotted a group of individuals with a massive high powered camera also trained on us. So much for security.

It's interesting to note, in all of our dealings with this type of activity, there was a pattern typically followed. Whether it was a loud brightly dressed individual being disruptive, or a black guy wearing all white, and "acting suspicious" - those were the individuals they wanted you to focus on. The real work occurred in the background with unassuming people dipping in and out, gathering intel. The two guys creating a ruckus were the ones they wanted us to focus on as a distraction. There could have been something being setup right next to us, but we would not have known. One thing which made this a bit more concerning than it normally would be, was the handshaking and handing off of the camera. That told me there were multiple groups involved, at least with this one.

Upon arriving home no one was there, yet all my doors and windows were wide open and there were what appeared to be foot prints on the floor made of flour. Just another message to tell me they were in my business, which I quickly cleaned up and pretended didn't happen. No sense in freaking anyone out by mentioning it, especially my family.

Another message they would send was the rearranging of furniture while you're out. It would have been nice if they also did the dishes and general help around the house, but apparently that wasn't in their job description.

The attitude of being under fire constantly sometimes made its way into sessions as well.

I am a very physical Viewer, but will also have moments where pure metaphor mixes with pure physical. Apparently my subconscious chose this tasking to go nearly full metaphor.

Within the session I perceived an African American male subject who was struggling against "The Man". Throughout his daily life, he was getting knocked down, chased, and watched suspiciously, though he knew he was doing nothing wrong. It was just who they perceived him to be superficially. The more they pushed, the more revolutionary and subversive he became. Then a bizarre thing happened during the session which had zero contextual relationship at the time.

As I was describing this, I quite unexpectedly jumped into a moving visual. I saw a very short film strip play out - I was looking down on a mailman strolling along a concrete pathway with a mail bag on his shoulder, and letters in his hand. He came to a door, opened up the screen, and on the door was a mail slot where the mail slides in. When the mailman shoved the mail through, there was a loud noise at my door which jolted me out of the scene. As I looked over, mail shot through my mail slot and onto the floor.

Apparently I had watched the mailman walk up to my door and deliver the mail in real time. It made absolutely no sense within the context of what I was getting in the session. Nonetheless, I wrote it down in my session, because within RV you cannot leave information out, no matter what you think of it.

When I received feedback for the session, it all made sense. I was to remote view myself 20 minutes into the session I was doing. Instead of describing myself doing a session, which would be very physical and representational, I instead used a metaphor for how I was feeling at that point in time. All the harassment coming from what I perceived as part of an authority structure, which I felt was completely unjust. Then the mail comes through the slot!

At this point it was 100% clear we were a target, and getting an investor caused a huge increase surveillance and harassment. Our sole job at this point was to make money so we could provide a return on that investment, but if we are getting blocked from making money, this venture wouldn't last long.

Unfortunately, we were up against a very powerful Goliath – because our remote viewing information on who they are reveals... well, let's just say that your tax dollars paid for this covert group to do these things.

Then the question comes as to why they are doing this. What's the reasoning for it? If remote viewing is declassified, why would those that declassified it try to shut us down?

Remote viewing declassification was meant to be a controlled space, and we were a loud wild-card within it, difficult to control and popular to a certain degree.

When it comes right down to it, we didn't need to remote view the who's and why's of it. Just the act of being harassed by an extremely sophisticated group smelling of covert ops should tell you that they take remote viewing very very seriously. The only thing they want from us though, is completely out, but we're not leaving anytime soon, because between the cracks some cool projects are coming through.

CHAPTER TEN
Project File -
The Amusement Park Con

In death throes, people and companies will turn to just about anything that can help change their current situation, and as such, we can end up being a last resort.

This was the case for a certain US company who created amusement parks and amusement park rides. With a large amount of high profile rides within very popular parks, they were one of the top developers in the United States, and branching out internationally to China when things went wrong and were facing bankruptcy.

They contracted with a businessman in China in order to build a park with rides focusing on UFO's and time machines. It was a monumental project to undertake, especially in a foreign country, and they needed someone who could move through the front and back-door business dealings in China as well as sourcing the materials and constructing the rides, while the US Company supplied the bank roll and the concepts. They arrived at a legal partnership and off it went.

The job went well in the beginning, at least on the surface, as the rides were being constructed. Once they were complete, the crushing reality hit home. None of the rides worked, or when they worked for a brief moment, they would soon break down. It would cost millions more to get them working properly, and there was no time or money left. The Chinese businessman had, unknown to them, stolen most of their money, while he built the rides as cheaply as possible. Shortly after, and when the US Company had realized what he'd done, he completely vanished, and no one knew where he or their assets went. They had been conned.

In the US they began legal proceedings against him for around 15 million dollars, and it went to court. Because he was in hiding, and not living within the United States, he did not show up, so they won by default. He was required to pay what they sued for, problem was, no one knew where he was. It was great they won the court case, but this guy was hiding outside of the US, and even if they found him, more legal proceedings may have to occur in the country he's in if he won't cooperate. If he's in China, paying enough people off to protect himself could conceivably occur, and they would never see a dime of their money again.

With private investigators, and even the FBI involved, they still couldn't find him, and the US Company was facing bankruptcy.

This is when they contacted us.

Our job was to figure out where he and the assets were hidden, then lead the client and investigators in, all with remote viewing.

A project like this appears fairly straight forward, and it is, but the big issue is trying to identify out of country locations where you could lead investigators. It's easy enough to describe his current location, but if investigators have no information on that location, it is very difficult to lead them there. You also need to be able to pinpoint where their money is, or what physical assets he's placed it in. He and the money could be anywhere within the APAC (Asia-Pacific) region, and since he is a con man, it's likely distributed, and under different names other than his own. We did know he had residences within China and Australia, so we were hoping to pinpoint him and the assets in one of those areas, Australia preferably.

We focused on China first, just to get it

out of the way, and through RV we found some of the assets in what appeared to be land with temples on it, but it wasn't the bulk of it. There were also various goods he purchased; gold, cars and jewelry, but it's still just a smidgen of what was taken.

As we kept digging, we found he was physically in hiding within Australia, which was a good sign because of potential issues with the Chinese Government in trying to get to him. Everything, from the bulk of the assets, to where he was, was looking more and more like somewhere within Australia.

Eventually we gave up trying to lead the investigators to his location, and even if they could find him physically, we needed to pinpoint where the money was. In our estimation, this would be his Achilles heel. If we could do that, and find a physical paper trail to tug on, he would come out of the woodwork no matter where he was.

One aspect showing up over and over when remote viewing the bulk of the assets within Australia, was an amusement park. It made sense because it was his expertise, and would be an simple location he could dump money into in order to make more. At issue though, are the amount of amusement parks within Australia, and trying to identify the one striking aspect which could lead us to it.

One description overlooked initially, and showing up frequently from one Viewer, was the word "moon face". It kept popping up here and there, along with general descriptions of a moon, throughout our probes into where the bulk of the assets were hidden. In remote viewing analysis, on the larger and unverifiable projects, there is typically one central idea or concept you need to grasp in order to line up all the data. It can take time to find this, but when you do, it all snaps into place and you have it. And that it did.

The one identifying aspect of this park is a moon, whether it's in the name, the city, or a feature of it. If we could identify that park, we may be able to come full circle.

It was even better than that, and it took zero time to know it. With a quick search online, we found within Sydney Australia, a place called Luna Park, and the entrance to the park was an extremely large moon face. That had to be where the bulk of the assets were hidden, and we were convinced there would be a paper trail which lead back to him.

The information was given to the investigators, and while not in his name, it was under a corporation he was connected to. When they began to make inquiries into this, he came running.

From there it was a matter of negotiating with him to get the most out of the judgment they won against him in the US.

CHAPTER ELEVEN
Counter Terror

Through the uncertain fog and haze on September 11th, I had a strong feeling we would be contacted after the Twin Towers fell, and I told others in our group the same. It wasn't a week later, the FBI reached out and pulled us into counter-terrorism.

The nationalistic fervor was intense, but we weren't necessarily sold by that. For us it was about the prevention of another attack, and saving lives if we could. We had also worked small projects for other people in other agencies, so it was almost to be expected that contact would take place. We also thought, perhaps the harassment and spying would let up because we would be working with the FBI.

When that first contact came, it was a

request to remote view the retaining wall underneath the World Trade Center. When the foundations for the buildings were constructed in the 1960's, they dug 70 feet below ground level and created a slurry wall to keep the lower Hudson and ground water out. After the buildings collapsed there was a massive amount of pressure on this wall, and they were concerned it could be cracked, breached, or about to collapse. If the worst were to happen, the first to get flooded would be the subway tubes, and after that, all of lower Manhattan. There was no way to send someone down there for a visual inspection because of the heat and debris, so they asked us what we could "see".

It was a quick project with a quick turnaround. We found it was intact and as solid as ever with nothing to worry about. Within a couple of days we had given the information to them, and they came back to us when they themselves corroborated what we found. It was probably somewhat of a test, somewhat of a double check...

The next request we received was to track Bin Laden through remote viewing in order to lead US agencies to his hideout, but we had an issue with that. One thing we did not want was collateral damage on innocent civilians by the dropping of bombs on a location we helped identify. Of course they would use many other intelligence assets to zero in, but something didn't feel right about it.

We declined the offer and instead we were asked to focus on counter-terror on US soil. These were more surgical and precise, from law enforcement raids to preventative measures, which sounded much better than blanketing bombs on a location. The main focus of this would entail identifying future attack scenarios, including methods and venues within the US by Al Qaeda or other related groups. The FBI was on pins and needles expecting another attack at any moment, so it was constantly relayed to us to work fast and thorough.

We had other projects to work on aside from this, but I needed to ramp things up to get moving. I still had to work through my daily remote viewing cue, while counter-terror related objectives were placed into it. I also had to task and analyze the data from the other professional Remote Viewers on this and other projects we were working on. Lastly, I had to get up to speed on every mode and delivery of attack they could possibly use - from biological, chemical, nuclear, conventional, plus all the methods of delivery for each, and all the physical effects on humans. This gets complicated and scary when you get into the biological and chemical side, because there are many different agents which create a host of horrible symptoms.

Downloading various types of information to your brain outside of remote viewing is important, because it's part of building an internal language. We are so used to conceptualizing everything in our world that we don't just experience what it is. For instance, if I look at a house, all I think is - "a house" - in order to save time and effort, but how would you describe it if you had no overall conceptual word for it? Would you even know all the materials and components that go into making one? How about different construction methods? If you have a building in a session, then you need to be able to describe everything at a basic level, and the same goes for the biological and chemical agents here. The more you have in your knowledge banks, the more you can pull on during a session and in analysis.

When you're researching and remote viewing chemical, biological, nuke attacks, and absorbing all the horrific ways people can die through these, you can get a little on edge. I would pray I wouldn't bi-locate during these objectives, because I didn't want to have intense experiences during these sessions. From bio to nuke to chem, unfortunately, I did bi-locate. With astounding clarity I saw what was happening to the innocents in the attacks, and it affects you in a negative way. This information is coming through your subconscious mind, and so it can deeply affect every aspect of you. Many of my days were spent shaky and racing through remote viewing analysis so we could get the information to the FBI, and there was clearly an edge of PTSD following me through these times.

We were chasing attack scenarios though, because they would constantly change.

The initial and main attack was multi-pronged with a sporting venue and subway/train event; the means of delivery both biological and chemical. The FBI wanted to know exactly what vent, and in what station the canister would be dropped so they could plug it up, and they did. They wanted to know what stadium and exact game it was, so they could provide extra layers of security, and they did. They were reacting and taking action on our information.

Under normal circumstances we would remote view, write up our findings for the client, and it would just be a matter of a few clean up details tasked out to the Remote Viewers as follow-up. Not so in this case. We would need to remote view the same question over and over at the request of the FBI - "The next attack on US soil by Al Qaeda or a related group(s)" because it kept changing, sometimes weekly. Then for every scenario we came across, we had to completely tear that apart to figure out every small detail.

We would notice within the RV data, the stadium where the attack would take place would change, probably because of extra layers of security placed on the last one. Then we would notice the method of attack would change, likely because something in their supply chain was disrupted. Then the scenario would completely shift, and we were on a different line than we were a month ago. We went from an internal chemical attack on a closed dome stadium, to an open air stadium with aerial vehicles spraying the spectators. Then it shifted to the poisoning of the food within the stadium along with the derailing of a train.

Even though the method of attack kept morphing, two things were very clear at the outset. They were looking to accomplish a multi-pronged attack, and they really wanted a televised sporting event. They weren't going to get it, because after a while, the ever-changing stadium attack drifted into obscurity, replaced by other modes and venues.

The next somewhat larger attack cropping up within our remote viewing, had to do with the creation of a mass of biological material intended for either the food we eat, or the water we drink, primarily within California. Within a remote location this soup was crafted with negative intentions, but we noted within the RV data there were so many environmental and scalability issues with this, that it was destined to fail, and it did.

They all petered out into a series of fractured events with no organized and sustained scenario coming forward. It appeared that once the stadium and train attacks weren't going to occur, there wasn't much of a plan after that, except for the nukes.

On the heels of the biomass concoction in our food scenario, and the one thing we never perceived with our RV data until cued by the FBI, were the suitcase nukes, and it's likely because it was layered deeper within the series of attacks they were concocting. We were always looking at the "next" one, and this was likely not slated to occur just yet, but we would have run into it eventually. As it was though, the FBI apparently had intelligence on these devices and that was when we were alerted to it.

My thinking around remote viewing the future was simplistic at the time, and it ran the line of - if I remote view an event occurring in the future, it's going to happen regardless of whether any action is taken on our information.

With regular remote viewing data, either current time or past, it's fairly precise, so I was just imprinting this line of thought onto future events. Overall, I believed it would not show up in the data if it weren't going to occur (or at least some rendition of it), but this is not so, and as we worked through this process, my thoughts began to change.

There was the overriding reality that we were preventing terrorist attacks from occurring, otherwise what use are we? The other side of the coin is, when you remote view the future, you are seeing the most probable outcome from your particular moment in time. As you get closer, things can change, regardless of whether the FBI was taking action on our information or not. This ultimately heads off into the realm of quantum strangeness, the double slit experiment, and the role of consciousness affecting the event itself.

There were a whole host of things to look into surrounding the anomalies of remote viewing the future, but things can roll fast, and we had some other stuff cropping up.

CHAPTER TWELVE
The Signal

12 people, a motley assortment ranging from business executives, feminists, tech workers, hippies, physicists, vagabond students, UFO nuts, and the occasional government spook thrown into the mix for good measure. They came from England, Australia, China, Canada, Russia, France, the US... They came from just about anywhere people lived.

The diverse menu was always the same for these courses, but they always had one thing in common. The need to take two weeks out of their life to learn how to travel the Universe with only a pen, paper, and their mind. It was a course where we would immerse and saturate select students with extensive remote viewing training. This was quite different than your typical weekend course because there is an effect that occurs when people remote view together in the same place day-after-day, for that long.

These courses were sometimes a circus sideshow of oddball personalities and behaviors. The barefoot 70 year old self-described "cult leader", with gray, smelly, shoulder length bedraggled hair, and long crusty yellow toenails snagging the carpet. Spying peanuts on the floor under the tables, he would swoop them up and eat them while simultaneously hitting on the 40 year old un-approving lesbian. Mind you, his swooping wasn't casually bending over and nonchalantly grasping. It was sitting under the table to eat it.

The uptight tech worker who believed he remote viewed someone's private parts. Drawing a picture of said private part, he taped a piece of paper over it so that no one could see it. Embarrassed, and slightly combative, he relented, and lifted the paper to reveal a picture of a large penis. Funnier than that though, was the objective had nothing to do with anything of the sort.

In his defense there is an interesting side-effect occurring during these courses, and it's very palpable, especially to those who are sensitive. Sexual energy has a certain feeling that is very easy to pick up on, and you can literally feel it expand and grow larger in the classroom as the days wear on. It's not really a sexual energy overall, it's only interpreted as that. It's a type of Chi energy generated by everyone remote viewing together. In fact you could often tell how well a course was going just by how many people were running off together. If at least two couples formed you knew this was a great class!

Did the two week course make people insane, or did they just show up that way? Aside from the UFO nuts, you never really knew, but one thing I did figure out rather quickly was that I was less insane than I ever thought I was, even with all of my seemingly crazy experiences with RV and beyond. On the other side of that, some real talent and amazing people came out of these courses, and some minds were completely blown open, never to crawl back into the box from which they came. Most everyone who came through one of our classes had an unequivocal "WOW!!" moment during the course. This was my inspiration.

As always, when we conjured a two week course, there was a heavy amount of push-back coming from the covert group in the form of increased harassment. It was an apparent issue for them, and they let us know, especially Pru, by ratcheting it up a couple of notches. I guess I came to expect it overall, but you would think it would be related more to the client work, research, or viewing future technologies that would push them over the edge. Instead, it was what two weeks immersed in RV did to the minds of these students. It rewired their brains.

You can see at a very specific point in these longer courses an energetic ripple beginning to move through the group mind, and one-by-one a transformation occurred. You can almost hear an etheric pop as each individual grasps a deeper aspect of remote viewing, with their accuracy increasing, and the subsequent effect it has on society as a whole - a 100th monkey effect. Dangerous indeed, to the ones that want to keep secrets.

There were two paths forming during this particular class, one was the instruction of new students to the world of RV and the other was arguably, a much more interesting one.

The first day of the course we received a phone call from Joyce Murphy, who at that time had a cable television show called "Beyond Boundaries". An unassuming Texan woman in her 50's, she would travel the world searching out paranormal mysteries, from UFO's to Cryptozoology, and lead investigative expeditions for anyone that wanted to join her.

By the look of her you would never guess this woman would be just as comfortable at a bar in a remote Central American village, as she would in a Texas suburb. Having gathered many sighting reports worldwide, she was a veritable encyclopedia of current paranormal happenings, as well as adept in the logistics of taking people to these remote locations. As co-host for this episode, Ruben Uriarte was to head out as well.

Ruben himself lives and breathes UFO's and is the Northern California Director of MUFON (Mutual UFO Network). Both of them were obvious choices for a TV show.

On this particular program with the Learning Channel, Joyce and Ruben were leading an expedition with a camera crew to Puerto Rico because of some unusual reports in a very specific area called Arecibo.

The Arecibo area of Puerto Rico is home to the very large radio telescope array SETI uses (Search for Extraterrestrial Intelligence), and it is featured in the film Contact with Jodi Foster.

SETI scans the skies for any noise and signals which could be construed as "intelligent" by analyzing any patterns within the frequencies. They postulate that any intelligent life forms out there in the Universe will be sending out signals we could potentially capture.

There were reports from villagers around the Arecibo area that colorful swirls and beams of light were shooting through the sky at nighttime. As well, local reported seeing on a consistent basis, a creature around three feet tall, scaly, large almond shaped head, red eyes, and frightful teeth... the fabled Chupacabra (A Spanish word meaning, "Goatsucker").

Ultimately, they wanted two things from us:

1. Remote Viewing information about the Chupacabra and where they could potentially capture one on film.

2. The nature of the lights people in the Arecibo area were witnessing.

With this as the backdrop, we began our project.

The Chupacabra

Lurking mostly around remote areas like villages and ranches, the Chupacabra stalks farm animals and sometimes even humans. With muscled hind legs that can leap through the air at frightful speeds and heights, it can be there one moment and gone the next, leaving its prey to die with vampire like puncture wounds and completely exsanguinated.

It has been witnessed regularly in Puerto Rico and Latin American countries since the 1990's, and there is admittedly quite a bit of controversy on the reality of it. With chickens and goats its main fare, and typically a lone peasant witness, I didn't put too much stock into any of it. Nonetheless we were tasked to remote view a good location where they could film one, along with any activity it was engaged in, but first things first.

When you craft an objective (what you want a Remote Viewer to view) you need to be very careful. As the tasker (the one who writes the objectives) you need to drop your preconceived notions about whatever it is you're trying to find information on, and work from the bottom up.

You can't just assume all those reports streaming in of a mysterious creature called a Chupacabra are true, because it could amount to a simple misidentification of some known animal, or a hoax. A seasoned Remote Viewer will let you know pretty fast what the reality behind the situation is. For instance, if you tasked a Remote Viewer on Santa Claus, the data you get back would have lots of language referring to mythology, culture and traditions, with no little to no physical representations. You understand clearly, and very fast, it is something made up. If the data comes back and the Viewer provides physical descriptions and behaviors with no mention of any mythology, or make believe aspects behind it, then you know you may have something real there.

I was, frankly, quite surprised when the sessions came back from multiple Viewers on the Chupacabra. All the sessions were very descriptive of this creature and its behaviors. There was no component at all to suggest this phenomenon was a hoax or not real, and we were digging hard to find it. We have run across many hoaxes when remote viewing supposedly anomalous things and events, so we wanted to be absolutely sure.

I recall one story we looked into where a person in the late 90's was on a hike in the mountains of Washington State with his dog. Walking a forested trail, the dog ran ahead of him, and when he caught up, a fight was occurring between the dog and an unknown bipedal creature. He witnessed, what he called an alien, tear his dog in half, at which time he claims to have hit it with a stick, killing it. From there he took the creature to his house and stuck it in the freezer, when soon after, some "military men" came and took it from him.

The person with the story was interviewed on many radio shows and wrote a book or two about it. We decided to check into the reality of his story and it was wildly different than what he claims happened. At the time this supposed event was occurring, our data revealed he was in a place like Las Vegas, or some kind of spa resort, drinking, scheming and concocting with a friend in a Jacuzzi/pool area. From start to finish, our data relayed it was a hoax, and the intention was to make money. I have to say though, I'm not sure how much money you can make hoaxing in the UFO field. Likely not a lot.

But for the Chupacabra, the Viewers described exactly what the people in faraway places were seeing and experiencing. One Remote Viewer even went so far as to describe with words and drawings how a mother Chupacabra chases, catches, and eats its young! All the descriptions recorded by investigators in the field were the descriptions we also got, and when your RV data shows up this way, then you likely have something real within our physical reality. It's actually harder to convince yourself it's real even though all the data points to that being the case, and much easier to come to the "it's a fake" conclusion.

As an interesting side note, many years later I was taking my son to school in Northern San Diego County. We were traveling on a rural road close to the house when we saw something strange. It was around 7am and there was a car just in front of us about a couple hundred feet. On the left side of the road, there was a small creature about three feet tall and tan to brown color. It was on two feet with large haunches, while the upper arms were like two smaller and slightly stunted T-rex arms. It was slightly hunched over and had what appeared to be spikes running from its head down its back. As the car in front of me passed it, the creature began to make its way into the road right in front of me. We were traveling around 45 mph so I had to slow a bit. It didn't matter that much because as it got near the center of the road the legs on the creature started to move so fast they completely blurred out, like the old roadrunner cartoons, and it shot off like you would not believe.

I wasn't sure what I was seeing and didn't want to cloud my sons head with my thoughts so I asked him to describe to me what we just saw.

His description was exactly how I saw it, and so I knew I wasn't hallucinating. If I had to name the creature we saw based on available descriptive information that is already out there, I would have to go with a Chupacabra. If I still did not believe that a creature like this could exist, I could now.

From there, we tasked various aspects of the Chupacabra in order to come up with talking points for the episode, but out of a quick curiosity, we tasked the Viewers on the origination point of this creature within our reality... in other words, where did it come from?

The Viewers described a jungled area, and within this location there was a large facility doing some under-the-radar genetic testing and... unconventional experiments. Apparently there was a bit of misfortune, because some got out. That was unexpected to me, but then again, I guess I didn't get too far mentally because I was still grappling with the notion they were a real thing. Of course none of this is readily verifiable, because we have nothing to back it up with other than RV work.

When you engage in RV projects that span verifiable objectives, all with multiple Viewers, you begin to understand how much you can trust your data on unverifiable objectives and projects. After a while your world view includes the unverifiable projects you have done and the conclusions you have come to. It's interesting, because RV is an experience where you actually witness an event or location, and when you combine that with corroborating data from other Viewers, it affects what you believe to be real and not real.

Ultimately we found this creature, or creatures, were getting very agitated in this specific region. We also found the normal "wildlife" in the area was acting up, with the agitation centering around the Arecibo Telescope array. Something was stirring up the local wildlife population, and it had to do with the second half of the project. The mysterious lights.

Incoming!

"They're coming!" An energy which felt like a wave of pods coming from space was breaching our atmosphere! It was as though they were hitting the steamy jungle floor, popping open, and strange beings streaming out of them. As I remote viewed this I knew that wasn't exactly correct, but it felt akin to that. These were coming from deep space with intelligent intent, and it almost felt like an invasion.

Digging deeper within my session and probing their mind, I found they had a very intense and acerbic intelligence, and they were here for a purpose. Add to that a very strong paraphysical aspect to these beings and I knew whoever they were, they were aware I was probing them. When you have lifeforms in sessions who are aware of you, they will sometimes unexpectedly drop-by for a visit later, which is somewhat concerning if you don't know their intent.

During the course of the class, along with the teaching of new students, I still worked through my remote viewing cue, slipping away here and there to do a session. Placed in, unbeknownst to me, was that first tasking on the nature/source of the lights the locals were seeing in the sky. I didn't know what to make of these beings which were associated with the lights, but I did know quite fast that the lights the locals were seeing had to do, in part, with them, and they were inundating the area.

This turned out to be a much larger project than we anticipated and went well beyond the scope of the Learning Channel piece, nonetheless, we relayed what we RV'ed at that time to Joyce and Ruben - which was they may be able to film some Chupacabra's around the Arecibo dish if they could get permission from the facility. Ruben and Joyce always did a great job on camera when the show finally aired, but I cringed when they mentioned to the Director at the Arecibo Telescope Array - "Some Remote Viewers from California said there are Chupacabra's running around on the dish; have you seen them?!" Honestly, I would have asked the same question as the host, nonetheless, it's kind of embarrassing.

As far as the mystery lights went, well there was somewhat of a rain check on that. We did tell Joyce and Ruben before they headed out that the folks working at the Telescope Array may know something is coming from space, but we hadn't quite sussed it all out yet. This event was much more profound than the Chupacabra's, and we had to get to the bottom of it.

We churned out hundreds of pages of data, with many Remote Viewers involved in the process, and it was a huge feat to analyze it all. We knew bits and pieces of what was occurring, but like any analysis project, there is usually one concept or central idea you need to find in order tie every single piece together. When it finally sunk in, it was 100% clear what all the data was saying -

The Arecibo array under SETI picked up an intelligent signal from space.

- SETI knew it was intelligent, but could not understand what the information was
- One individual at the array was studying it outside of their normal working hours
- This individual was trying to show others what it was, and when the government found out about it, it got swallowed up and disappeared
- The witnesses on the ground were seeing both the lasers from the array, and lights these beings were creating as they came to

Earth

- The lasers coming from the Arecibo array were used to measure distances so they could understand where the signal was coming from
- These beings, are the signal and they are not the signal. They use the signal in a sense to travel here. They pulse themselves within it from a location in deep space.
- The energy of them coming in to this area was causing an agitation within the wildlife population, Chupacabra included! That is the reason for the uptick in sighting reports
- The location they are coming from, and the signal, is likely High Velocity Cloud W491

It was amazing to me this particular SETI outpost was receiving an intelligent signal. Like the Chupacabra, I hadn't considered too much around the SETI effort, and had always wondered why they were looking out there, when there are a lot of anomalous incidents occurring on Earth itself. It makes you wonder how many other intelligent signals they have captured and buried.

So what are we to do with that? It can be mind-blowing and earth shattering to people, but not many out there really believe what some crazy Remote Viewers have to say. I can run around yelling that SETI received an intelligent signal, but unless it comes from an authority figure, no one will believe it. All we could do was to place our report on the website and keep going forward.

Thus began the waning desire I had to want "UFO", or "Alien" disclosure from those who guard the vault. From my own personal experiences, I can say I believe there are other lifeforms from other places and dimensions visiting Earth. There is also an incredible amount of amazing evidence which would win a court battle of "others" being here. As individuals, I think we can all know for ourselves on a personal level if we wanted it.

Indeed, what was to follow this project showed me even more that individuals are the leading edge of contact. I had mentioned previously that some beings will pay a visit when they take notice of a Remote Viewer probing them, and this was the case from this project...

CHAPTER THIRTEEN
High Strangeness Incoming

Dead space. A vacuum all around me; an indescribable ocean of blackness. Not the mundane kind of blackness where you close your eyes and see nothing, but an infinite multi-dimensional, darker-than-black expanse whose tendrils reach and travel forever. My head was spinning and tumbling like a piece of space debris caught in orbit trying to get its bearings straight. Every once in a while a colossal blue globe would quickly pass my field of vision as I tried emphatically to halt this dead spin and focus in on it. It was the only shaky consistency in my world that I could try and grasp at that moment, being that I couldn't remember how I got here.

Then the obvious occurred to me, well, how did I get here? Closing my eyes I sunk deep inside myself to probe for something I could grasp onto, but memories seemed like an impenetrable bulwark; a giant brick wall I had to find a way into for an answer. Hitting this wall repeatedly couldn't be sustained and I contemplated just letting myself go into that infinite void of infinite black substance, leaving behind any effort.

As I was about to slip away into this ether, I began to remember something. It was an alarmed voice and an image of my wife from earlier in the day.

Seated at the dinner table with eyes wide, tracking back and forth, she's staring past me down the hallway that leads to the living room.

"Um, what is that!?"

I can see the deepening concern on her face and her eyes frantically trying to pinpoint something in the dark space behind us. Quickly craning my head back behind me I catch the tail end of "something" meandering like a lazy Sunday drive down the hallway. It was an ephemeral trail of white and light blue sparks ensconced in a translucent milky substance, like a train of moths spontaneously combusting one after the other.

My mind is straining in an instant trying to put it together with a palpable source, one that explains without any doubt the house is on fire, or perhaps, a bug zapper was left in the hallway. Just as soon as I saw it, it was gone, and there was no bug zapper, nor was there a burning house. I looked back to her; fear, relief and questions running over her face. My mouth opened, chewing out a slow drawn word, "Moths?"

Like traveling down a dark tunnel at the speed of light I found myself right back in the spinning vacuum. This time my face slammed against a porthole window, my whole world leveled off and I was completely lucid and aware. I was staring down at our Earth from space with its fragile layers of atmosphere and white wispy arms covering parts of her continents. Pulling myself from this awe, I looked to my immediate surroundings. There were exposed colorful wires everywhere, a skeletal framework and a control panel in front of me. Like a space monkey, I was in some sort of pod floating in orbit and in that instant I knew what was happening. It all came back to me.

After the incident at dinner we were both very tired and felt an uncharacteristic heavy pull to go to sleep. What was it that she made for dinner? Was it the pasta? Did she slip me a mickey? Ah, fuck it... so tired.

Drifting off quickly, I found myself almost immediately in this scenario, now fully aware it was a dream and what I was supposed to do.

I was stuck, trapped in orbit. I came up here to look for something very important and it had to do with a project we were currently working on. I knew that my team, my Remote Viewers, were down on the surface of the planet waiting for me to find it, and available to help if I needed it. I called down to them using some 1950's radio relay system built into the ancient control panel in front of me... some remnant left in my psyche from watching too many reruns of Lost in Space. "Danger Will Robinson, I'm stuck up here, I can't find "it" and I can't get back. Please get help, call on whoever you can to get me out of here, use the communication protocol!"

At that moment I realized they didn't have to do anything because out of my port-side window I could see a huge object moving toward me. It was glowing and shaped like a large brain, or a chewed up wad of gum which somehow exuded an acerbic intelligence. Watching it intently, it appeared to be a giant hive of some sort with streams of electrical blue lightening zipping across it and beings inside of it. I knew just the act of expressing the need for help inside of myself called them to me.

Back in bed, while this theater is unfolding, I am starting to notice someone is tapping me awake; pushing on my shoulder harder and harder. I try to brush it off because this so called dream is too enticing to let go of. The incessant tapping continues and I mumble "ok ok", assuming it's a complaint about me talking in my sleep again. Better make it fast so I can get back to this lucid dream.

I reach around to grab the hand that's tapping me and I get a sensation of a strange slick bumpy surface as it pulls away. I'm startled, I sit up straight, jolted into complete awareness with what feels like gallons of adrenaline finding any and every avenue of expression through my body in one instant. In front of me is a three foot tall "thing" with a head shaped like a football on its side. The eyes are two small peering black dots on the far ends of this angular football shaped head. Overall, it's a light tan color with darker brown spots and right under the head are a myriad of large bumps. The rest of the body appears to be a spindly mess, barely capable of supporting this large head, yet it moved with such ease.

My body seems to be having a visceral reaction to the presence of this thing that appears to be nothing mammalian, reptilian, mineral or vegetable. Primal physical fear consumes me and panicked emotions flood into my head. All sorts of ingrained coping mechanisms are trying to assert some control over my body and mind, but it is not working!

As I am trying to cope with this mess, I hear clearly in my head: "Don't be afraid. I won't hurt you. We are here to help you and we would like you to help us. We made your dream. We are from the Signal."

At that moment while "it" was saying this, I understood and felt from this creature all of the emotions occurring in me were like rocks being thrown at it. The intensity was too much for it to take, so it started backing up and waving its gangly limbs frantically. While making an audible "noooooo" sound, it disappeared into an explosion of zipping blue fireflies.

This was the visit I was half-expecting after crossing their path during the work we did on the mysterious signal, but I never imagined that the weirdness quotient would ramp up this much. There were too many questions here, but the main one was, what project, and what could I possibly help a race of beings with, who appear to be extremely sophisticated?

CHAPTER FOURTEEN
Moving to a Zen Center

No matter how hard a mortician tries, a body still looks dead when it's dead. The rosy cheeks and pasty makeup can't make up for the fact that there is no energy in the body. I was meditating, sitting on the floor next to her, the old teacher Lola Lee-Osho.

I had known her since I was a child and she became a big part of my life, being the teacher at the Zen Center. Her beginnings on a spiritual path were shrouded in some mystery. Part guru, part bare bones Zen teacher, sometimes when I would speak with her in sanzen (the private meetings you have with your teacher during meditation periods), she would all of sudden begin to shift and move - without moving a muscle - to a position floating above my head as I sat in front of her. I would be looking up at her, but it wouldn't register until I left the room. Always confused by that, I would begin to feel a lightness of being, and powerful energy move through me. For most who worked with her, these events would happen, and it's somewhat of a field effect which occurs if you work with a guru. They seem to have an energy which can transfer to student, causing strange perceptions to take place, or brief "enlightenment" experiences.

In the 1920's, 30's and 40's before Zen came to America, there were spiritual movements, which were a combination of different Eastern and Western practices and philosophies all jumbled together. From speaking to the dead, to mystical Christian practices, to Indian (guru) type practices, as well as magick initiations, they fell somewhat under the moniker of "Spiritualism" and were the forerunner of today's New Age movements. Lola's underpinnings in spiritual life came from this. Loaded with a lot of mind bending and useless philosophies, there is a lot to get stuck in your head and ego with. If you can make it out of your head and philosophies about it, and into more of a meditative practice side, deep revelations can occur along with a cultivation of a lot of energy.

When she became a teacher, likely in the 1960's, one of her students owned a large chunk of rural land in Northern San Diego County where Azaleas were grown. The owner gave a slice of five or six acres to the forming group, which she was a part of, and they built a structure to meet and practice meditation regularly.

As life progressed, Lola began to incorporate more Zen into the teachings and practices when she connected up with a Rinzai Zen Temple in Japan. Many of her students traveled there to take part in meditation, my dad included. Because Lola hadn't received her "realization" or abbot-ship from another Zen teacher as an heir, the center was still somewhat on the outside of the whole Zen system and lineage, yet it had become the sole practice there.

My parents became involved during the late 70's, early 80's, and they would take my brother, sister and I to play in the thickets and trees while they meditated. I could feel even then, the land and what the people were doing was somehow special.

The meditation hall sat in an ancient oak forest and it was circled with these sentinels protecting it. I would sometimes climb the trees and spy down through the window at the meditators on their cushions, wondering what was happening inside of them. Later, I heard Native Americans practiced vision quests in the area long before white people settled it, and it made sense, some places just hold a vibe like that.

When you die, there is a certain amount of time where the body needs to rest. All the energies of the deceased person need to make their way out, and burying or cremating the body quickly after death is not as supportive to this process.

During this rest period, chanting services and meditation around the body help the person fully detach and leave. As I was alone and meditating with Lola's body, there was not one ounce of "her" left inside of her; nothing hanging on at all. She was gone, having likely let go a long time ago with her realizations there is nothing to hold onto, even in the midst of living life. Death forces you to let go of life and everything in it, but her practice and where she went with it took her to a place where she had already let go, and was just in the moment. I was sad she was gone but knew she was fine. It was more about me and my concern for what would happen to the future of the Zen Center she established and ran for decades.

Within spiritual traditions and especially Zen, there is often an heir. This person takes over the teaching and guidance at the temple, but no one in the group had broken through to a point where, in her estimation, they could do it. So the group was left hanging, but continued to meet and practice diligently. Tani-Roshi from Japan took a small interest in taking over, and made some trips out, but he ultimately declined. It was all because there was no real lineage at the center and it wasn't completely connected to a Zen temple system in order to keep it going. Someone had to step in to pull everyone along, but it couldn't be just anyone.

I had begun to focus more on my life in Orange County after graduating art school, and didn't go down to the center too much after she died. The only other Zen groups were of the Soto style, and I didn't feel much resonance to them even though I tried. There is a Japanese saying: "Rinzai for the Shogun, Soto for the Peasants". It's reflected somewhat within each style, with Rinzai being for the warrior class in Japan, and Soto for the commoner. In other words, the discipline is more intense on the Rinzai side and I was more accustomed to that. Rinzai also uses a koan based approach, as opposed to the shikantaza practice Soto uses.

Koans are basically riddles the thinking mind cannot solve. "What is the sound of one hand clapping", or "Show me your face before your parents were born" are examples of some of the first ones you encounter. They cannot be answered by "thinking" about them and coming to a conclusion. The answer comes from somewhere else, and you need to show this answer to your teacher. It's a whole system to push you out of the thinking mind into an enlightenment experience and expand your awakening once you pass through the initial koan, while shikantaza (what Soto practices), is "just sitting". Value exists in both, but there was more of an edge and bare bones feel Rinzai had, and I missed that when I started jumping around the various Soto centers.

Of course here in the West, any formal Zen training can be different and not as intense as what occurs in Japan because of societal leanings. The Japanese culture has a different way of doing things, and what would be OK with them is quite often not OK with us. They are a culture with a built in tendency for intensity if you look at their ancient and accepted practice of formal seppuku. Nonetheless, it is intense on a internal and personal level.

You are required to sit and meditate (called zazen) without moving for periods of 30 to 50 minutes, then 10 minutes of walking meditation, then back to zazen. Depending on what's happening at the temple, this typically occurs in sets of three or four, 30 to 45 minute periods, which will last up to two hours total.

During the time of sesshin though, things ramp up a bit. Sesshin literally means "touching the heart mind", which is a period of intense zazen and silence. It occurs at various times throughout the year and can run from two to seven days, while you sit on the cushion eight to 10 hours daily.

You can't just get up and leave either, nor can you fidget while on the cushion. If you decide you're done and leave before the meditation sessions end, then you are really done, and quite often can't come back.

There is someone called the Jikijitsu who wanders the room with a long flat stick called the kiausaku. Silently walking up and down the aisles of meditators, this person looks for fidgeters, dozers and others who need a whack or two. Sometimes you hear snoring, and that will always be cause for the Jikijitsu to get up and give a wakeup call.

The whole purpose of sesshin and the practice in general is to slow and stop the monkey mind. All the random thoughts we twist and turn with, to the emotional wants and desires keeping us spinning in suffering. In fact the basic tenet of Buddhism is that life is suffering, but if you follow this path (zazen meditation), it is a way out of it. When you are able to do this long enough, and it is different for every individual, something can happen called kensho, or satori, and we translate that as enlightenment - seeing into one's own true nature. There are no books, there are no readings that can take you there, only going deep inside to find the answer which exists outside of thought, and no thought can grasp.

It's not that there is anything to "teach", or that you even need a teacher. Of course there are writings but they all have to do with inspiring one into the practice as opposed to any belief. There is no belief system in Zen and that is why those from other religions, like Christianity or Judaism will get involved, so they can deepen their understanding of what is being "taught" through those religions.

I believe the very core of all religion is to look deeply within and drop your beliefs instead of creating more, even though it seems the opposite. All that truly occurs in Zen, is talking students out of their trees so they continue practicing meditation. Whoever takes over, would have to had plummeted the depths in order to show the way through the eye of a needle; a rare and hard to find person.

The center had finally reached out and connected with Philip Kapleau-Roshi, who wrote the quintessential book on Zen titled "The Three Pillars of Zen". It's a book nearly everyone in Zen ends up reading, being one of the first in-depth books from an American who came to enlightenment through the practice. Because there was no one who was able to take over the teaching, they asked if he would, or knew of anyone who could. One of his heirs, Mitra Bishop-Sensei was willing and able to do it (at that time she had "Sensei" appended to her name, which means teacher, but now she is Roshi, which means "Great Teacher", so I will refer to her as Roshi from here on out). She had a very small monastery in the mountains above Santa Fe New Mexico, and had also become an heir to Shodo Harada-Roshi in Japan, another clear and great teacher. She arranged to go back and forth between her monastery and the Zen Center, conducting sesshin, and running the temple. At that point I decided it may be time to go back down and see what she was all about.

Mitra was the wife of a diplomat during the fall of Saigon when the US military finally evacuated the embassy at the end of the Vietnam War. During that period, she was back in the states while her husband and two sons were at that Embassy. She had no idea whether they had died in the evacuation or made it out, and didn't know for quite some time, having become estranged from them. Deciding to pursue an intense spiritual path through Zen, she had left her family in order to live at Rochester Zen Center in New York where Kapleau-Roshi taught. I can only imagine the intensity of the daily suffering she must have endured during this period. Fortunately, being a diplomat, he and his sons were the first ones out, and made it safely back. Given the length of time before she knew anything though, must have made it much harder to deal with.

I found her to be very clear, focused and integral, so I decided to begin practicing there again.

Not long after I was going back and forth from my home in Orange County to the center to meditate, the benefactor who gave the original piece of property, passed away. She was a long time member, from the very beginning, and much to the chagrin of her children she willed all of her property to the Zen Center. In total, the center now owned just over 30 acres, and they needed someone to live on site and take care of things, so they asked me.

Moving there was a fairly easy decision. My wife at the time wanted it to happen, and having a two year old son, it would be great for him to live in a place where people practiced deep meditation, along with open fields for him to explore, instead of concrete. I did have a nagging feeling deep within me there would be a negative impact at some point on my marriage with this decision. I had also heard how couples who engaged in these practices together seemed to split up more than the ones who didn't do this together, which seems odd, but it is the case. The other side of the internal argument I had was my drive to go as deep as I could within myself, and that made it all a no-brainer.

We had gotten married while we were both getting our degree in Fine Art. A very creative person, she was also engaged in a meditation practice, but not to the degree that I was. During art school I would routinely head to the Zen center in order to practice as well as go to sesshin, and she became involved in that with me. In fact, just after we got married, we spent a week at sesshin meditating.

Obviously this was not a normal monastic situation, nor was this considered a monastery.

This was a lay center, and was the reason why I could live there with my family, work professionally in a remote viewing think tank, and engage in a much deeper meditation practice. I was required to have other duties as part of my job - the contact for the center, opening of the building for practice, administrative duties, plus general upkeep and maintenance of the property and buildings.

For better or worse, we made the move.

John Vivanco

CHAPTER FIFTEEN
Project File -
Computer Company X

For many great inventions or scientific discoveries, there was a "psychic" behind it.

Sitting in his chair, he relaxed his body and mind until he drifted into that realm where visuals about anything can be accessed. With a single question in his head, or his tasking, he was seeking an answer to a problem in need of resolution, and he was dropping down into "theta" to find it. When he came back, he had an answer to his question, and was able to move forward with an invention.

This was how Thomas Edison used "remote viewing" and he wasn't shy about telling people. What did he call it though? "Accessing the subconscious mind".

His method was to relax in his chair, in his hand he held marbles, and under that was a pie tin sitting on the floor. As he drifted from his normal and awake mind state he held a question, something he needed to know in order to move forward with his invention. He slipped past beta, then alpha and finally hit theta, like we all do when we go to sleep. Once in theta state where hypnagogic images come, he sees the answer to his question in full visuals. Inevitably he would drift off into delta, which is full sleep and where the memory of what occurred in theta gets washed away. He knew that muscle control is lost in this state, and when that went, so did the marbles into the pie tin, and he came back into full consciousness with the sound and his solution.

From the cure to Diabetes, to the makeup of Benzene, to great archaeological discoveries, the scientists behind these used similar methods like Edison in order to access this place of knowing. Einstein, Marconi, Tesla, and many others used it and even spoke about it. How is it that a scientific community will accept that, but not remote viewing when it comes to solving issues they face?

Remote viewing is applicable to every industry and subject matter you can think of. There is nowhere it can't be used and nearly any problem can be figured out with it.

The best situation for a remote viewing

professional is to work with an engineer or a scientist directly involved with the issue they are working on. That way, you can get their years of depth and knowledge on the subject to help in the process of analysis. Sadly, the world of science does not believe remote viewing is possible (for the most part) and this is why that back door is the only way we can get in. It's interesting to note though, if I dumped the term "remote viewing" and removed the stigma of "psychic" from it, the acceptance would be higher.

It lies in the definitions of words, and that is it. Accessing the subconscious for information or being psychic, there is no difference between what Thomas Edison was practicing and what is called psychic functioning.

I think the research and development side of many high tech companies could use, or hire, a team of very specialized "subconscious idea generators". Would that make it more acceptable than "Remote Viewers" or "Psychic Spies"?

When faced with a problem a certain computer company came to us, and it was once again a back door deal, because, as psychic spies, we were too sexy for our shirts. They had only begun to figure out, like Sony and some others, this type of "problem solving" can make the difference between losing and winning. At issue was a new computer line, just on its way out, which was crashing consistently just after boot up. It was the whole line, and the problem could not be isolated by their engineers so it was up to us to find it.

The issue arises when you, as a remote viewing professional, have no expertise in the area you are working in. In a perfect world, the Viewer would just describe it as it is with all of the sciencey nomenclature so it's easily figured out, but often times they don't. Rather, it's metaphor, similes, concepts - a lot of "it's like this..." That's when it's useful to have someone on the client's team to help you try and understand the data. Even though we had consistent information from the Remote Viewers, and the help of an engineer who could isolate the general components, we could not find that single concept to explain it all.

I decided to try a different method to figure this out, and one that Dr. Frederick Banting, the Canadian physician, used to come up with the cure for Diabetes. I would access it through the power of dreaming.

I wrote on a piece of paper, "describe the reason why the line of computers is crashing", and stuck it under my pillow before going to sleep.

I found myself in a dream where I was chasing Nazi's around a dark grocery store (no idea what that means!), I suddenly remembered the issue of the computers and I stopped and said aloud, "this has nothing to do with the computer issue!" Once I said that, a Nazi ran up to me with a wadded up piece of paper. I opened up the crinkly mass, and scrawled upon it was, "induction". I said ok, stuck in my pocket and began chasing the Nazi's again.

I had no idea what induction meant having never needed to know, but when I looked up the definition, it was right on. There was electromagnetic induction occurring between components that the Remote Viewers were ultimately describing. It once again came down to that one single concept needed to tie every piece of data together. Induction occurs when one component receives electricity and there can be a wave, or magnetic flux, coming off it. Within computers, if this is not checked, then it can cause issues for other electrically charged components. In their case, it shut down the whole system, but with this revelation and all the session data on it, they were able to fix and launch the line.

John Vivanco

CHAPTER SIXTEEN

The Quantum Strangeness of Future Terrorist Attacks

Think of time, events and dimensions as a band of undulating colors. It moves, twists and flows in a way where the shape constantly changes. When remote viewing the future, you're trying to grab a frame, or snippet, so you know how to react before it happens. The problem is, this band of colors keeps flowing out of a hole of unknown probabilities you can't see into. It keeps pouring out and undulating even after you've grabbed your snippet and straight up to the time of the event. The hole from which the band of colors comes from doesn't even know how it's going to turn out. Add to this, the potential effect of placing consciousness, or remote viewing the event, and it can push it in unexpected and different directions.

This was the case for the many attack scenarios we were picking up on at the request of the FBI, but suitcase nukes on US soil was very concerning because it wasn't a potential grabbed out of the ether of future possibilities, it was based on intelligence relayed to us, and the authorities fear of detonation. The word was, there were at least three, maybe four located in cities across the country, and they knew the location of some, but not all. If one were apprehended, the others would receive that information in an unknown way, then move into position and detonate.

We worked to identify where the "lost" ones were with as much physical detail as possible, all the way to the exact city of detonation. We also needed to understand the method of communication if one was apprehended, as well as descriptions of the terrorists. From their physical makeup to consciousness mapping, where they worked if they had a job, descriptions of their houses, etc... We had such good physical descriptions of them and the others outside of this scenario, that we requested access to the Fed's database so we could line everything up more easily, but they wouldn't let us in that far.

Remote viewing all the angles surrounding what's happening in real time is one thing, because they are already occurring, but they also wanted to know what the future held, which opens the paradox door.

One way we would dig into this was to remote view "the most significant event on US soil conducted by Al Qaeda or related groups during the month of such and such". We would work this angle, month after month to see what we could see. Most of the time it was just arbitrary low level situations, like threats or maneuvers conducted within our borders, or media announcements about them. Nothing big, and nothing to be concerned with. It was about three months out, though, from our current time we noticed something significant was taking shape.

Remote viewing the future is not unlike the <u>double slit experiment</u>[i] - an experiment in quantum physics which shows that a photon (a light particle – see endnotes) will act like a wave and a particle at the same time, which is a contradiction to the dualistic mind. When you try to observe, or measure the experiment, the behavior of the electrons will change. It appears consciousness affects it, or creates the reality of the measurement.

To top it all off, a single photon will interfere with itself once it goes through two slits creating what's called an "interference pattern". That is a paradox because it implies the single photon, before it heads through the slits, goes through all the possibilities of itself going through the slits. This is, in part, where the multiple universe theory comes from because in order for the single photon to interfere with itself, it's thought it would have to encounter itself from other dimensions in order to do so.

Where it's akin to remote viewing is on multiple levels.

Picture the whole experiment as a "remote viewing the future" experiment. The single photon is a course, or a trajectory of an event you want to know about in the future. Pretty straight forward. But the photon as it moves forward in time, goes through all the possibilities of how it could end up, and it displays all the probabilities as a wave function. Some of the possibilities cancel each other out, some are emphasized, but they are all there.

In the experiment something funny happens when you place an observer in the middle, which is akin to the Remote Viewer observing the outcome of a future event. What happens, is the wave function collapses and now the photon acts like a particle, giving only one possibility. It can also cause a different outcome than what you expected.

In the context of terrorist attacks we began to see a large scale incident occur in the not too distant future. Our Remote Viewers were describing a highly energetic event in a port city related to terrorist activity. The signatures of this energy came back as being nuclear in origin and it completely decimated an area of important commerce. The more we dug into it, the more concerned we became because the situation was not changing, like the others, and it all came back to a suitcase nuke detonation. We rushed a huge box of data and our reports off to the FBI while we held our breath and plugged our ears.

Can Remote Viewers "see" the future? Of course they can, but that particular future may not occur. With the other attacks we reported on, they would change, and I believe it was because they were mostly thwarting them through our RV data and other intelligence, along with a bit of quantum strangeness thrown in. With the nukes though, I'm not too sure what occurred, because nothing happened and they never passed information back to us.

The Farsight Institute (a remote viewing group), did a study in conjunction with Glenn Wheaton's group HRVG (Hawaii Remote Viewers Guild), and Lyn Buchanan's group. Their study was to determine future climate changes on a city-by-city level. One of the locations they tasked was LAX Airport six months out from their current time, to see what sort of changes had taken place. The Remote Viewers described total devastation, and not because of the climate, but because of a massive earthquake. They surmised it must have been in the 9.0 range, or possibly even higher to create the destruction they were seeing in the data.

They published the information online, and claimed there was a possibility of a large one six months out. The time came and there was no large earthquake, other than a 5.0 quake in that time and region. This happens, your data is 100% clear, but you get to the event time and it is similar but different, or, it does not happen at all. We already know what to expect with regular and verifiable data, so something is clearly off sometimes when you dig into the future.

In order to try to understand what was happening, they set up an experiment just to see if you could remote view the future. The way they did this was to separate the tasking time from the viewing time. Normally you would think of, and write up, an objective before you give it to the Remote Viewers. Instead, they gave the Remote Viewers the tag to do their sessions on, but didn't write up an objective yet. All the Viewers sent their data back encrypted so no one knew what was in those sessions. One month after the sessions had been done, the tasker looks for an event that happened from her point in time, back to the time the Remote Viewers did their sessions, then tasks the one month old sessions on it. Of course, they are all very accurate and descriptive of the events they tasked on, experiment after experiment.

Their supposition is that the Remote Viewers are able to accurately describe the future from their perspective in time. Courtney Brown, who ran the projects, came to the possible conclusion of multiple universes. He postulated the Remote Viewers in the original LAX data did view the future, just not in our time line, and the 5.0 felt in LA, then, was like an echo from another time line where it was a 9.0.

While it's an interesting experiment, I don't think you can completely infer Remote Viewers can see the future from this. I think what's clearer is that the untasked and encrypted Remote Viewing sessions, were existing in a state of probabilities before becoming tasked. Once you have someone who wants to "measure" them, is when the wave function collapses and you form the reality. In this case they can be totally correct because you know the event already happened.

I am digging myself into a huge hole of Quantum Mysticism here, but as far as separate time lines go, there is no way to know, but it could be. If you remove the time line theory, what you have at a basic level is, Remote Viewing can only give you the most probable outcome from where you are in time, and this outcome can change based on many impacting factors as you move toward it. Notwithstanding, placing the Remote Viewers as the "measurement tool" in the quantum realm can add more unexpected outcomes.

That aside, we have done many future prediction experiments where they were correct. I remember one was an unexpected outcome with the presidential election between George Bush and Al Gore. Within our data, there was no clear winner at election time, which was extremely confusing. We also saw a couple of months after the election, it was determined to be Bush. That seemed like a very improbable situation, yet we still published our data, albeit apologetically. It turned out it was too close to call at election time, and it took until the end of the year to determine a winner.

From the chem/bio attacks to the nuke, nothing happened. In the whole scope of things, the only information we received from the FBI was purely related to operational matters we needed to know to complete our job. In other words, they didn't tell us, "oh hey, great job, we were able to thwart this and that attack based on your information". There were no tea time conversations, but we did see later news reports with statements from the FBI on potential attacks they knew about, and they were directly related to what we remote viewed, except for the nukes.

So what happened? Why didn't this, or any of them make it into our reality? Is it because the consciousness of a Remote Viewer can affect the outcome, like the observer in the double-slit experiment, or could we be viewing other time lines? Perhaps it's simply that they were able to stop these events from occurring based on our information and others, but I suspect it's a bit of all the above. One issue I have though, those nukes were never in the public mind, and if they captured them, you would think it would be a coup they wanted the public to know about. They may still be out there.

John Vivanco

CHAPTER SEVENTEEN
The Firefly Aliens

Like a giant brain floating through the sky, with blue electrical veins zapping across its surface, it is at once a single intelligence and is also a ship and portal that contains and transports the aliens from the Signal. I can feel their whole paraphysical mind, like a wave passing through me. I can also see small individual aliens moving out of it and closer to me. They are coming, and letting me know this, behind my closed meditating eyelids. I crack them open to the light, and I see blue sparks floating and popping all around me.

"I hope no one else saw that", I think. I'm currently in a week long meditation retreat, sesshin, but these beings are trying to communicate with me full-force telepathically. I know most here meditating have eyes slightly open and focused downward, but if the Jikijitsu catches wind, he could come over and smack me with the kiausaku.

Strange things can happen while you're meditating, and because you meditate. Often times I am the Jikijitsu, and in that position, during certain periods, you will walk around with the kiausaku in order to keep the energy and discipline up. I would often see things happening in the room and around the meditators, like flashes of light or colors, sometimes even visuals from their own mind. Typically I'll just ignore it and move on, but sometimes I'll get a sense they need a bit of prodding in a different direction, or an energetic wake up call.

I am used to beings flitting past my consciousness, trying to grab my attention, so this wasn't unexpected or scary in any way. There is a fine line between what you think you are creating, and what is coming from somewhere else, like I realized early on with remote viewing.

Once, while doing Kundalini Yoga, a being came to me in a panic. It was standing in front of me waving its arms, yelling "John, John, John". It was frantically trying to get my attention so I stopped what I was doing and politely asked it to step back and wait until I was done. It's somewhat of an annoyance and pet peeve of mine when one pushes hard for my attention when I'm busy. Home is also my sanctuary, and unless invited... I get testy. About 15 minutes later I am interrupted by my phone ringing. It was my mother in law (at that time). Apparently, her Mother, my ex-wife's Grandmother, had just died 15 minutes ago. She was coming to me because she didn't know what to do. I went back, found her, and helped her transition by calling on some of her relatives who had already passed.

The pressing continued so I reluctantly decided to see what was wanted of me. When sesshin begins, I usually don't communicate with anyone. I can easily do this after, and what I am doing on the cushion seems more important than spending time in the ethers. I was also feeling very conflicted about doing remote viewing, or working on the "outside" at this point in time. Normally people drop most aspects of an outside life when they live in a place like this, and I was beginning to think I should do the same.

As I shifted attention, ready to receive and communicate with words and mental images, there was an excited clattering coming from these beings.

They immediately launched into my consciousness, and I began to see hundreds of them streaming from this large brain like intelligence sitting just outside of Earth. There were flashes of mottled skin as they approached, like brown and tan patches on a dog, and large ball like bumps under the sideways football shaped head. They told me the softball sized protrusions under their head were specifically related to being able to shift into other dimensions. From the changing appearance they mustered; flashes of light, telepathy, to pure physical, they are able to traverse our reality and others.

They gave me the understanding that the radar array at Arecibo picked up on them, and they were emitting a similar signal across multiple frequencies, when combined, could be construed as intelligent? At least that is my limited understanding, and is probably mostly wrong. I do know something happens energetically when they move in specific ways, which emits a signal and a sound. They also relayed that the pulse of the signal contains them, and they move as if in, and part of it. When they arrive here, in a sense, they get off the Signal.

There was also a juxtaposition of personality with them. As a whole, or group mind, there was a very sharp and cutting intelligence. So much so, it was somewhat intimidating. When there was only one individual with me, it was a totally different sensation and experience. As individuals, they would sometimes refer to themselves as "brown hounds". In other words, they were playful, sensitive, kind, and full of joy. It was as though they reserved the pure intelligence aspect of themselves for the group mind.

Now all around me I wondered if anyone else in this sesshin sensed them. It is often that beings from other places come in and observe what we do while in sesshin.

Once during a sesshin at our sister Zen Center in New Mexico, it was as though an intergalactic bus would pull up and drop a bunch of beings off when we would do the daily chants, morning and afternoon. It was a very small group at this particular sesshin, just me, the Roshi, and my mom for the week.

I was the densu, lead chanter, and as soon as I began to hit the bells and begin, you could hear and sense them come through the front door and skitter down the hallway. My perception was that they were very tall beings and there were a load of them. Hundreds, if not more. They crowded into the very small adobe zendo (meditation hall) and gawked at us while we chanted. As soon as it was over they would noisily skitter back down the hallway, jump on their bus, and be off. The next chanting ceremony, it would be the same. For seven days this occurred twice a day.

Everyone in that sesshin, the three of us, all noticed, and commented on it after. If they arrived before you were on your cushion, which they sometimes did, you had to squeeze through them in order to get to your cushion.

I thought perhaps this could end up the

same, yet with the focus on me.

In my mind's eye I saw flashes of jungles and creatures within them. Not the "dangerous" Chupacabra laden jungles of Puerto Rico, but somewhere else. I saw Christmas lights flashing on and off, on and off, all in unison, then it quickly shifts to fireflies doing the same within a humid jungle. They impart a sense of imperativeness and the rush to do something because they are in trouble. They let me know that this is the project they want us to work on with RV.

Fireflies? In trouble? What does that mean? Is that what they wanted to tell me? I didn't really have time for these wanderings in my brain, so I placed it on a mental shelf and went back to doing nothing on the cushion, but after that evening's zazen was over, things took a strange turn.

During sesshin, we end around 10pm then back on the cushion in the zendo at 4:30am, so you don't get too much sleep in general. Unless you're going to be meditating late into the night, people generally try and rush off to bed.

My quarters were behind the zendo, but you had to cross through an ancient oak grove, then a bridge traversing a seasonal stream, and then through another field and finally the walk to my door. It was a roundabout way to get there as this bridge was not a direct path. Once across the bridge and away from the oak forest all you had were open fields and starry skies.

As I came to the transition point from forest and bridge, to field and sky, I began to see something. It was a flickering light high up in the sky. Clearly not an airplane because it was stationary and flashing blue and pink, nor a star because it was too big and bright. I stopped and gazed at it for a minute, when all of a sudden it was like someone flipped a switch and the whole sky began to dance with color.

As if on cue there appeared everywhere above my head flashing colored lights in all different colors and sizes. Some spinning in place, some moving around quickly, some stationary. Some looked like mini-galaxies, and some looked like siren lights flashing. It was as though the movie Close Encounters of the Third Kind came to visit me. It was the most unbelievable and amazing display I have ever had the privilege of experiencing, so much so, I thought I was hallucinating. I wanted someone else there, someone else seeing this with me, but there was no one around. Everyone was off and going to bed. As much as I shook my head and rubbed my eyes, it would not go away.

After a bit of time it began to taper off and I noticed something out of the corner of my eye within the small overgrown orange tree grove by my house. There were probably 12 orange trees crammed into a space surrounded by thickets, and dotted within the orange trees were five very old and very tall pecan trees. I thought my eyes were playing tricks on me, an after effect of the display in the sky, but within the grove there appeared to be some erratic blue flashes.

It was dark and the grove was even darker, so there was a bit of hesitation. Some areas of the property were downright creepy with things lurking and watching you, and this grove hugged the edge of one with a dark cloud. My house was on the other side of this, so a walk past it was unavoidable. It's one thing to have the safety of miles between you and the lights, but this removed that perceived safety layer and I could see the leaves and oranges light up repeatedly and very briefly with a blue tinge.

You hear people speak about seeing small orbs of light close to them during and after some UFO displays, and as I moved closer and closer to the grove, that is what I saw. Zipping for a couple of seconds, forming small streaks and then disappearing, or hovering and making a slow bounce through the air before dissipating, they were everywhere in the grove. They looked like blue fireflies, but there are no fireflies here, and there was no insect left, once the light disappeared.

Then I realized what this was all about and who it was. This was just a different aspect of the Football headed aliens from the Signal.

As I gawked, I wondered if they would again show up in their pure sideways football headed madness, with their little hammerhead shark eyes. By this time I had no fear because their energy was clean and good, so I felt like I could take it without throwing my emotions at them.

As they spun and flashed in the air, I could begin to sense a pressure on my consciousness coming from them. At first it was feelings and senses that this orange grove is where they will "be". A place they would come through, and a place I could connect with them quickly and easily.

Then the communications began to get clearer, and I could hear distinctly that they did not come here to interact with humans and had little interest in us, but I stepped in the way and they were not expecting that. Their ultimate intent is in communicating, interacting and helping other species on Earth. This was an interesting message because we normally assume, "aliens" are here for us humans. I've come to know there are many different types here, and for each one there is a different reason. Why should it always have to do with us?

They have some type of connection with the fireflies here on Earth and that's part of the reason they are here. So, instead of calling them "Sideways Football Heads", or the "W491 Aliens", it made sense to call them the Firefly

Aliens. I do not know what they call themselves personally, but this was the closest they agreed we could get.

Before this encounter with the Firefly Aliens I have had run-ins with others. Most of the run-ins are of a different ilk though. Many of them, like the ones known as the Grey's, will subdue and mollify the mind of the human they are interacting with.

I ran a remote viewing project once on the reason why they subdue the mind and I also sent Viewers to the "most benevolent being/alien that uses the subduing of the human mind method and to describe". It's pretty obvious as to why they would subdue our mind and bodies, and the remote viewing data reflected this. We are like wild animals to them, and it's akin to a lion getting a tranquilizer dart from a human so that we can take something from it or study it.

What I found really interesting though, were the sessions on the "most benevolent one who does this". The reason I chose the most benevolent, was because I didn't want any Remote Viewer to end up getting visited by something negative, and I thought this would suffice. Talk about ego! The being was described as a priest by the Remote Viewers, but the reason it used this method was that it felt as though it was "above", and better than us. It used it for our own good, it said. Not one Viewer who did this session liked this being because of how pompous he was.

This is a marked difference between how the Firefly Aliens interact with me. They are upfront and do not use this method because they respect us and are of a higher vibration. With the first encounter I had with them, I felt stressed out and emotional during it, but they did not mentally subdue me, as some others would have. Instead they let me know my emotions were too intense for them, yet still interacted with me in an upfront way. They set the space so I could grow and understand how to create better contact with each interaction.

What I ultimately came to realize is that any species who comes here and subdues our minds, and erases parts of our memories in order to deal with us, are not our friends. They are only out for themselves, no matter how they try to explain it.

Things were tapering off quickly in the orange grove, but it was clear the display in the sky and in the grove was meant to get a deeper introduction going. They also wanted help, and I may have put off a sense of incredulity surrounding the issue of fireflies being in trouble. Not so much now, though.

Nonetheless, my current priority was sesshin, so I left in order to make the early wake up call.

CHAPTER EIGHTEEN
Project File -
The Treasure Hunts

It just gets embarrassing when you add "treasure hunter" to "psychic spy", and if you were ever going to wear a cape, this would be the time. At least in my youth, *The Goonies* and *Raiders of the Lost Arc* shaped some fanciful expectations in my head of extreme adventures and unearthing incredible relics. While the adventures are there, it can be very difficult to do the unearthing.

Within the Southern California desert, there are a trove of stories and legends of lost treasures and mines. Whether it was from the Spanish, stage coaches, a lone prospector losing his mine, or underground cities with riches and giant mummies, it's not difficult to suss out with remote viewing whether anything is there or not.

You don't want to go chasing them without first vetting it with the Viewers, and we found many stories are just tall-tales. It's also an effect of the "telephone game" where the retelling through the years has sent it in many different directions, some innocent, some on purpose. Then you have the legit stories, where treasures exist on land which is inaccessible through protection acts, or military bases, etc... Inevitably, that leaves a small sliver for the intrepid Remote Viewer to base an adventure around.

Fortunately, we have two things out here in the So Cal desert, (where we would mostly hunt) a frequently robbed stage coach line, Spanish Missions and lost mines.

A huge interest of mine were the Spanish, and the lore surrounding their exploits in the New World. It was often that they made their way up the coast, or inland through the desert with a load of riches, to be deposited at one of their established Missions. They would often run into issues with the Native Americans and lose their horde, or a ship would sink. Within the Mission system, which ran the whole expanse of what is now known as El Camino Real and Highway 101, there were vaults and places of safe keeping for these treasures until they could get it off to sea and back to Spain for the Crown. Some of these vaults were even located under the pews within the main chapel or directly underneath the altar. The one location god-fearing Christians would never desecrate.

There are locations within the California desert where you can actually find markers for old Spanish caches and mines. They followed a strict system of carving on trees and rocks so they could get back to it, or tell someone in the know, that a trap was waiting. From cyanide to a purposefully collapsing entrance, it could be your suicide if you venture inside one of these unknowingly. More often than not though, these signs were geared to lead you astray.

The Spanish also engaged in the gruesome habit of murdering someone, sometimes even two, and burying them with the treasure. Laying them to rest vertically, standing up straight within the ground, with guns or swords drawn on either side of the treasure, they believed the dead would protect it in the afterlife.

There are many different aspects to hunting treasure, from picking the right one, to knowing what the laws are. You can't just traipse in and start digging in federal, state, or even private land. For private land you need the permission of the owner, for many state and federal land it's just a no go, except for perhaps BLM (Bureau of Land Management) land, but it really depends on the location. Even relics beyond a certain age are restricted from getting dug up. When we were set up, they were counting on us not knowing the laws, or playing to our sense of greed. Fortunately Pru had carried herself with integrity and wouldn't be drawn into something like that.

There are many locations within the California desert that hold quite large caches. One of the biggest in my estimation could be one which lies within the vast Borrego Desert.

The general story tells of a group of Spaniards crossing the desert with up to eight cartloads of gold and jewels, taken by their exploits across the New World. As they were skirting an enemy Native American encampment they were attacked, but in the midst of battle they were able to hold them off long enough to bury it and hopefully survive to retrieve and continue forward. Unfortunately, the last Spaniard was killed, and with that the true location of the treasure died with him. How this makes it out and into a story, especially when very little written word could account for it is beyond me, so you have to start at the beginning.

The very first thing with any treasure story is knowing the reality of it. Is there anything there? Is the story real and correct? Often times we find the general idea behind the treasure is correct, but the story and location are wrong.

We remote viewed the reality of the story and the reality of anything being there. Often times the stories still get passed around after someone has found it because there is rarely any publicity surrounding the find, or there was nothing there to begin with. Not that I agree with this, but one of the credos for treasure hunters is that you pull it out on the darkest, rainiest night of the year, and never tell a soul.

The initial sessions came back, and surprisingly, there were gold bars, Spanish coins, jewels, gold crosses, even swords and armor. It did not appear there were eight cartloads, nor even six... maybe two or thee tops, but it's still a huge haul. The story did have more of an exact location where it should be, but that was not correct either, based on our data. We saw this stuff was located in a hole, and as the sun passed overhead, the light would penetrate into the hole and actually hit the goods. With a flashlight, it was conceivable you could easily spot it.

From there we went about looking for the landmark, natural or artificial, closest to the treasure with remote viewing. This is the way in, and it's usually bright and huge, so much so it's a WOW moment when you're out in the field and you're able to line up the data with the real world.

On one occasion I was looking for a cache of coins taken at gunpoint from a Butterfield stagecoach run up to San Francisco (The Butterfield line was established as the southerly mail and transportation route where it ran through the Southern California Desert before heading up to San Francisco, and it was robbed frequently). The lore on the location of this particular buried treasure covered a huge expanse of desert, and based on the story, it appeared getting close was nearly impossible. I tasked Pru on the problem of the landmark and the location of the coins.

With the initial session, I had her remote view where I needed to go when I was out there camping. My plan was to spend the night in the desert, and once I set up camp I wanted direction from that location, and what I needed to look for.

Being blind to my tasking, she described a subject (who was obviously me), completely confused on the route to take, at which point he simply raised a pair of binoculars to his eyes. After that, all she wrote was: "look for the red, look for the red!"

The next tasking I had her do was a landmark I could easily spot close by the cache. It was an extremely short session with desert washes, and it said "Hollywood Blvd" on a street sign. I wasn't sure what to make of that! She was prone to describing things in a highly conceptual way, so I thought perhaps it was metaphor for a major road out there. The problem was, there were no major roads out there, except for the highways, and they aren't exactly like Hollywood Blvd.

When I settled into camp, I was completely lost on what to do, so I pulled out all the project data. From the lead-in landmarks to the descriptions of the site itself. I remembered

Pru's red spot and confusion, so I grabbed the binoculars and scanned the massive expanse of desert before me. When you're at home remote viewing, collecting data and looking at maps, it can be easy to get locked in the myopic perception it won't be too difficult to find it. Once you get out there with the sheer size of the desert in front of you, it hits - total confusion, and that is exactly the position I was in.

I placed the binoculars to my face and back and forth I scanned, trying to find something, anything. On the side of a mountain, probably 15 miles away, was a very large red mineral deposit! This must be what she was seeing. At that point, at least, I had a direction to go, so I pulled out the maps and planned my route to get as close to that location as possible. The other bit of data she provided, which was a landmark closer to the treasure was a street sign. The only problem was, if I were to take her "Hollywood Blvd" as a metaphor and ascribe that to the major highway cutting through the area, it was nowhere near that red spot, and I am 100% sure there are no roads out there called "Hollywood Blvd", at least not on the maps. In fact, there was nothing out there at all except brutal desert back country and very few dirt roads.

The next day I set out to make my way to no man's land and made the transition from the lonely paved highways, to the even lonelier dirt washes and roads. I decided to ignore the street sign in the data, and just try to get as close as I could to the red spot.

A couple miles in on a rough dirt road there was a very large mound where the road split and went around each side. Choosing the right side of the road to make my way around this large pile of sand was when I saw it. Unexpectedly, and my mind blown completely, there was an actual street sign jutting up from the side of this pile of sand which said "Hollywood Blvd", and absolutely nothing around for miles.

For the Spanish treasure as well, the landmark was pretty unequivocal in the description by the Remote Viewers. It was a large pipe near a big hole in the ground where a mine once was. The Viewers described this large pipe coming out of the ground, and because of hard flowing water, there was desert plant debris wrapped around the base.

On the esoteric side, the Remote Viewers were approached by a very large Native American ghost in relation to this Spanish treasure. We connected with him multiple times so we could understand any dangers, in other words, if we had the dreaded treasure curse. He was very slow and deliberate in his communications when I and other Viewers encountered him, and he was iffy on the protection side, because it did not seem his energy was present enough for that. One request he did have was a monument of some sort to the ones that died in the battle once it was retrieved.

His life was an interesting one, having been taken by the Spanish as a slave to guide them and help communicate with other natives, he became more and more attached to his captors. So much so that even though he was released at a certain point, he stayed with them, fighting and exploring alongside. His attachment here was just a piece of his overall energy, or soul if you want to call it that. Sometimes only a small portion of energy is left behind in an attached state over an unresolved event, while the rest moves on to other lives. If it were a full bodied and energetic spirit, then we would likely have issues. Anytime we encounter these unresolved situations, we help guide that stuck portion back to where it needs to go.

It seemed to be enough to make a trip out, so I loaded up my gear into my 4WD and headed out.

Through washes and desert terrain, a 4WD is a necessity when making these excursions, otherwise it's a no go. Having spent about six months in the mountains of Arizona beforehand and exploring alone nearly every day just for the fun of it, I knew the risks and dangers of getting caught in rough terrain where there is no one for miles. You need plenty of food, water, extra gas and tools for when and if your car breaks down. You have to be able to survive for days on your own if something goes wrong.

For miles I drove into the area where I thought the treasure could be, based on the remote viewing data and the stories surrounding it. One mile in a 4WD on rough terrain seems like forever, and I had gone quite a few more than that, having taken a back route so I could be as stealthy as possible. This is an area where smugglers bring Mexicans and Central Americans seeking a better life (as well as drugs), and there are constant rounds by the Border Patrol. If the Border Patrol didn't spot and harass me, I could get hung up having to deal with smugglers, which I didn't need. The route I took would likely skirt that kind of activity and I would hopefully avoid any trouble.

As I'm driving this route, I'm beginning to feel I made a mistake and I'll never come across my landmark. The road is not really a road, but a broken and narrow wash with sections of soft sand to get stuck in, and fissures where the truck put all it had into its articulation to get through. I was always just a hair from getting stuck for good, and walking out would be a nightmare.

Finally, as I rounded a bend and dipped down to cross into a major wash, I see it. Within a massive water shed with debris caked around it, just like the Viewers had described, it was right there in front of me. A single pipe jutting from the desert floor about 10 feet in the air and barely visible from outside the wash because the sides were so high. I got out of the car and immediately found a deep black hole going straight into the ground to a depth unknown; the abandoned mine, which was also described by the Viewers.

I knew I was close.

Following the data, I made my way on foot through the washes crisscrossing the desert floor, some very deep and some shallow, looking for the hole the Viewers described it as being within. My only issue was, which fricken hole was it?! Before me lay thousands and thousands of holes where the water from the summer thunderstorms violently raged, finding all avenues through the soft sand and into a wash. To add more danger and obstacles to the mix, you never knew which hole was going to house an angry rattlesnake, as I found out by sticking my head into one. Coiled and ready to strike, it would have latched onto my face if I hadn't jumped back in that split second. Note to self, never stick yourself in dark holes in the desert.

With RV and treasure hunting, there is rarely any issue getting yourself to the location. The lead-in landmarks are always there and easily identifiable. The issue is how do you identify that very specific spot where the treasure is hidden. A Viewer can describe nearly everything about the treasure, get a massive amount of detail on the surroundings, even great descriptions of where it is. The Viewers will describe a uniquely shaped rock, or a tree that's got a bend to it, or a swath of colored dirt, but when you get to that level/location out in the field, everything is unique! You need to have many different types of equipment to and try identify the exact location, because the descriptions will only get you so far and won't tell you the exact spot to dig. You can dig a massive hole and find nothing, yet be just a couple of feet from it and never know.

CHAPTER NINETEEN
Firefly Project

I was still a bit incredulous regarding the fireflies being in trouble and how I could possibly figure out where this may be. How can fireflies be in trouble, aren't they ubiquitous?

It turned out to be a two second search online.

In the dark and lush jungles of Malaysia, where the tides of the ocean push and pull on the Selangor River, there is an ecosystem in perfect balance and where Pteroptyx tener lives, the synchronous flashing firefly the locals call the "kelip kelip". It's not that there aren't others in the world who flash in unison, there are. They only sync every once in a while, with a couple of synced-flashes in between the un-synced flashes. This particular species, which lives in only two known locations on earth (the other being the Brazilian Amazon), is always flashing in unison, and their habitat along the Selangor River is in trouble.

In tropical areas where the tidal flow of the ocean and rivers output meet, you get a narrow balanced band of salinity and fresh water, where specially adapted creatures and vegetation thrive. The unique species who live here are more or less dependent on this mixture of fresh and salt water. If there is a disruption in this, from development, to chemicals, even too much or too little rain, you are going to have issues.

Traveling down the river at night you would see the Berembang tree lit up like Christmas with the firefly flash communication occurring in sequence. Being a mangrove specific tree, it's used by the kelip kelip as their display tree and is quickly disappearing because of the strains and stress on its ecosystem. The life cycle of the kelip kelip is actually quite short, with the time spent as a beetle and flashing on the tree a mere two weeks. Overall, the firefly lives around six months, but most of that time is spent as a larvae eating snails in the detritus along the river banks. Once it becomes a full-fledged firefly beetle, off it heads to the Berembang tree to mate and then die.

At issue, was a large dam being built upstream on the river, as well as extensive clearing of their local habitat for agriculture and other uses. The dam would cause a decrease in fresh water flow through the mangroves, and the balanced ecosystem where the kelip kelip live would get thrown off balance. The agriculture, with the clearing of land and the chemicals dumped into the water, was also at issue. These two together create the perfect storm and apparently have far reaching effects, beyond even our 3D world.

It's an interesting concept; the potential demise of a species would affect something else outside of our Earth world. I had never gone that route of thinking, or ran across this in the past so I wanted to understand what the relationship was between the aliens and the fireflies on earth.

We had located their likely location within or near the High Velocity Cloud W491. On the edges of the Magellanic Cloud, these bodies are extremely large gas clouds on the disk of our Galaxy, moving at a higher rate of speed than other masses around it. They are full of dark matter, baryonic matter, and all manner of star making material. As they race through the Galaxy they contribute a load of material to the creation of stars in the Galactic Disk.

At the time when Arecibo received the intelligent Signal, SETI was using a program called SERENDIP (Search for Extraterrestrial Radio Emissions from Nearby Developed Intelligent Populations). This program piggybacks on more conventional operations within radio astronomy, and the telescope was trained on this particular High Velocity Cloud at the time.

Being doubtful there would be much of anything sentient there, I was a bit reluctant to task, but we had to in order to clean up the edges of the project on where the signal was coming from. I was surprised when the data lined up between the location the Signal was coming from and High Velocity Cloud W491. From the Viewers we received descriptions of alien intelligence and a pulsing signal coming from within it. They even described "The White House" knowing about it, and were very concerned with the implications.

As individuals within the species they all have their own unique personalities, yet as a whole, they are able to pull one very intelligent mind together in order to accomplish their goals. They are at once physical and non-physical, able to use the 3D world we are focused in, as well as the non-3D and paraphysical world that we humans argue the reality of. This is why they can show up as physical creatures, to blue lights, as well as communicate telepathically. They straddle the worlds consciously - they are themselves, and they are the Signal that some underground government agency is likely still trying to decipher. We had, in fact, tried to contact someone within an agency we had no connection to in order to help guide the process of unraveling the message, but got no response.

I suppose the reaching out we did in order to help was somewhat of an invitation to them, and like certain projects in the past, I noticed an increase in surveillance and suspicious people wandering the very rural property I lived on. At the same time, my computer was hacked and my hard drive destroyed in the process. When these incidents occur we always need to know the reason for it, and who's doing it, so we can figure out what action to take, if any. As expected, it was a military agency we had never had a connection with, and they were looking for information on this signal.

These aliens are intrinsically linked to the synchronous flashing fireflies on our planet and for whatever reason, if the fireflies go from here, so does a part of their world. Somehow they are genetic cousins and there is something the fireflies here on Earth provide for them. We all have our paraphysical aspects, but there is something about the fireflies and their flashing that goes much deeper than our Earth reality. It's as though the flashing pokes out of the fabric of our reality and into theirs. They utilize something the fireflies create in a dimensional and energetic way. It is somehow part of their world in a very important manner and there is a disintegration occurring because of it. As the life of these fireflies drain away, so does an aspect of theirs.

I really can't claim to understand this though, because I am limited by my own human language in trying to relay concepts, which I have none for. It is often the case when you get into these types of projects where you cannot effectively communicate in a way that satisfies both sides. While this side is not clear cut, the issue of the fireflies in the Malaysian Jungle is - their habitat is getting destroyed, and what can we do about it?

Unfortunately there's not a lot we could do about a dam being built, because it was a government project and exists on the other side of the planet. Governments tend to do what they want regardless of negative effects, and in this case it was clearly going to be built because of the crony-capitalist setup they had. At least in the US, the government tries to hide it somewhat, but in Malaysia it was akin to the President approving the dam, and his brother building it. A lot of inside people would make a lot of money, and the momentum was too strong.

The catchment area of the dam was going to completely flood ancient native peoples land and sacred sites, in fact, the Orang Asli had to be relocated from a place they have lived for centuries. The Department of Geology also recommended against this dams' location, because the substrate was too loose... the list went on and on, with very credible reasons as to why this particular dam should not be built. The World Commission on Dams, which is an arm of the World Bank, even made the statement regarding this dam: "while dams have delivered significant benefits, in too many cases the price paid to secure those benefits has been unacceptable and often unnecessary". It has to tell you something when the World Bank will make a statement like that, then deny funding on a major infrastructure project like this.

With remote viewing we looked at a number of issues and resolutions surrounding it. The main point the sessions relayed was the dam will be the major demise of that ecosystem unless there can be mitigating factors. Whether it is a waste of time or not, we had to look into how it could be stopped.

Because there was a lot of back room dealings, and the price securing the benefits of this particular dam extremely high, the Remote Viewers described the creation of a documentary exposing this. People love fireflies as well. They remind us of the magic we felt when we were kids, playing hide and seek on a warm summer night, watching the thrill of bugs blinking in the dark. This goes for any person in any part of the world. I don't normally think people would even consider that a firefly species would be in trouble, but the documentary would need to cover the magic of these beetles, and especially the curious and endangered kelip kelip. The Viewers stated, that if we were to combine the magic of the beetles along with the back-room dealings in a documentary, it would "stop the project dead in its tracks".

That was not to be, as we could not get it going and pull something like this together in the time frame before the dam would be built, even though we tried. We had media contacts here and there, and we pushed on them as much as we could. The main issue was, TV is based on entertainment and ratings, and that's it. They only care to place money behind ideas that they know they'll get a return on. In these days of reality television, people have gotten so used to hollow and concocted drama or watching blind hillbillies without teeth battle alligators, that a simple documentary on fireflies just didn't do much for the excitement factor.

In some of my later work on TV, I did a show for National Geographic about remote viewing and treasure hunting, and the "campfire stories" from the producer and crew were always interesting.

One cinematographer I worked with related a story about a *Big Brother* type show he had worked on. There was a relationship formed during that show on camera between a male and a female contestant. In order to spice things up a bit and get some drama going, the producer of that show had one of the crew members place another girl's underwear in the guys bed, so his new girlfriend could find it. I suppose we could have had our wacky team of Remote Viewers talking crazily about aliens and the relationship to the kelip kelip, but I wasn't that brave.

Ultimately, it would have been the case where we would have to fund it and try and sell it to a cable channel, or send it off to Sundance in order to get any play. It makes it even more complicated that is was on the other side of the world from us, because we would have to take into account how to connect with the Malaysian people, which is culturally a world apart from us.

The only other thing we could do as a mitigating factor, was something I was beginning to pull together on the research and development side of remote viewing. A very esoteric and energetic way to approach these issues. The Environmental Healing Protocol.

John Vivanco

CHAPTER TWENTY
Remote Healing & Influencing

"It happened again" Pru said. I asked "what happened again?" "Another death threat! They said, stop what you're doing or we'll kill you; all of you". "Ok" I said, "let's get together and talk about it".

It had happened to me, as well, while on the phone talking with a friend. Click click click, the line started to make a lot of noise like someone was picking up and placing a receiver back down. A menacing voice crashed the conversation ... "We are going to kill you if you don't stop this". Click, then gone. My friend left wondering asked - "Why did you say that!?" Me ... I am watching the window, expecting assassins to come swooping in at any moment.

They would always follow up with a nice

round of remote influencing in tandem, so the point was driven home. The red haired step child of Remote Viewing, Remote Influencing, or RI, was developed by the military later on within the remote viewing program.

In the historical accounts of military RV, there is a story where they were using it on Saddam Hussein literally 24/7 during the first Gulf War, in an attempt destabilize him mentally, so we could depose him from power. They were unsuccessful, but it became part of the deep lore of remote viewing, and we knew it all too well.

RI is meant to manipulate an individual, and has the potential to push your thinking and feelings in negative ways. It's a subtle and esoteric process where someone trained in it can move thoughts into your head which are not your own. The ultimate goal is to make you do something they want you to do.

With the constant remote viewing I was doing, as well as ongoing meditation, it was easy to tell when there was someone else pushing on my consciousness. Not just with RI, but also straight remote viewing.

There had been incidents before this where an individual would suddenly appear in my mind's eye and I would sense an intrusion on my being, their intent to gain information and influence me in some capacity. Because I was aware of it, there was not a lot they could do, and so it was ineffective. In particular a woman with dark hair and haunted eyes would come before my mind's eye as she tried to menace me. Somewhat similar to a ghost, but I could feel the connection to a body she currently had. This person was part of the team assigned to try and contain us, and in fact, I found out who this person was in real life. It's a sad situation when your job is to try and harass people who are interested in opening people's minds to their own possibilities. Using RI for mal-intent toward anyone will actually affect the one doing it more than it will affect their target. You have to become darkness in order to give darkness.

We had done what is called "Remote Healing" which is the more happy and benevolent side of this whole influencing business, and I did notice it does affect the mind of the recipient. As you do RI or RH, you could feel what was occurring within the mind of someone who is on the receiving end. As you're transferring energy, or thoughts into a subject, you could sense their mood begin to shift, but to nearly all people, this is something they are not consciously aware of.

We had a couple of locations where we would meet up and talk business related issues, and this time it was a library in order to discuss the threat. While we were in the middle of our whispered conversation on what to do, we both suddenly froze. Something very strange and palpable was beginning to crawl up on top of us. There was definitely a bout of RI coming on, but this time it was a bit different; it was a wee bit stronger.

In fact, it was not subtle at all, and it felt like a very black energy was trying to get inside us from out of nowhere. A dark and foreboding sense crawled under our skin, beginning at our feet, working its way up our bodies, and tried to wedge itself into our minds. It was hard to shake, and it was meant to spark severe fits of irrationality and general instability, so that we end it all out of fear. In that moment the overwhelming sensation I had was that we were about to be killed.

Backing physical death threats up with this, can be an effective way to really drive it home. One time, I had even gotten the energy of the one who would assassinate me driven into my mind. It's a strange feeling to know there is nothing personal about it and the job would be done with clean precision and a "sorry bro, but it's my job".

The ultimate problem (from their end) was we were aware of being influenced. If it were done to people who were unaware, then you may be able to influence them to the point where they make unconscious decisions. In this particular instance it was so intense, they may have also used a technological aid. If you've even been in an area where there is an extremely high amount of electromagnetic energy, it can have a similar effect of fear on the brain.

Anyway, it was a nice try on the back and forth Remote Influencing skirmish side.

On the happier side, RI can also be used for good - you can use it to heal people, animals, even environments and species. In fact, we used Remote Healing quite a bit and the results were often tangible.

There is a different protocol for RH and RI which can be used as an adjunct to a regular remote viewing session, or used exclusively, depending on what you're doing.

What does healing mean? For the body it means it is in a sound or healthy state. For instance, if you have a broken bone, then it would be mended and functioning well. The thing is, if you have an idea of using RH to mend that bone, you could create a worse situation than what is there. What if the person with the broken bone needs to go through a process which is outside of a straight and quick healing, which you are intent on producing?

How about someone with a terminal illness, and they don't want to die? Do you try to heal that illness so they can keep living? What if the healing they need, and are subconsciously going after, is death? You can't assume what a situation needs when you use any type of RH, so you pull back and give the energy which will help for their greatest good. This gives them the energy for a healing to take place according to something much deeper, and in line with their highest intention. In fact, it can often run counter to their conscious desires. When we would work in this capacity with people, you would see things change, as it would bring whatever energy they needed forward. Even the word "healing" is somewhat of a misnomer, because there is nothing to heal.

Aside from humans, I had created a protocol to deal exclusively with environments and species called the Environmental Healing Protocol (EHP). The protocol is meant to bring the resources and energy into environments currently in an unbalanced state. Sadly, this typically falls under a "due to human activity" situation, whether pollution is killing everything, or people are taking too much from an area, affecting a wide swath of biology.

In part I had created this in response to the firefly issue in Malaysia, as I knew it would be a serious long shot that we would be able to get anything going on the media side fast enough.

Much like conducting RH on a person, you can't assume an environment needs to be a certain way in order to be healed, and so you work through a protocol which works with it in the way IT needs to be, as opposed to the way you want it to be. Maybe it needs to be unbalanced in order for other situations and species to take root. If this is the case, you'll know, and the proper energy will come forward for you to use.

There is an algae called Caulerpa taxifolia which has decimated areas of the Mediterranean Sea, and continues to do so. Dubbed the "killer algae", France, Spain, Italy and Monaco tried but could not control its spread. It literally takes over areas by blanketing the ocean floor, effectively killing off all other organisms. In the Mediterranean, it grew from a square yard to 11,000 acres within a number of years, and created economic and ecological devastation.

Originally found in tropical climates, it was introduced in the salt water commercial aquarium world because of its fast growing and decorative qualities. Unfortunately, it made its way out of someone's fish tank and into the ocean where it continues to wreak havoc in the cooler waters.

In Carlsbad, California it was likely someone had decided they would release their unhappy fish from their aquarium into one of the local lagoons. Instead of just the fish, it was the whole tank, killer algae and all. Because of the Mediterranean climate the devastation can be severe if it makes a very short hop, skip and a jump into the ocean at large from there. Conceivably it would wipe out all the local life on the ocean floor and become an ecological disaster equivalent to what is occurring in Europe. The scientists who began investigating, and working on the issue in Carlsbad, expected this would be a major disaster, as there had been no way to control, or stop this from happening in other areas.

Being local, we took an interest, and aside from remote viewing the general "how to get rid of it", we also employed the EHP. The protocol works by bringing all the fruits to bear on balancing a situation as opposed to something specific, so in a sense there were no judgments on what needed to occur for this balance to take place. By working the protocol, the effects in the real world can run the gamut from something magical occurring and the issue disappears, to human resources solving the issue. It's meant to add energy for the quickest and best way in order to re-balance.

So we began the process of the EHP on the lagoon, and at the time we started, things were not looking good, as it was spreading out of control.

At a certain point in a series of these sessions, I could feel the balanced energy begin to lock in. Amazingly, in a very short period of time the biologists actually created a new system to eradicate it, which fell in line with our conventional viewing on how to stop it. Somehow, huge leaps and bounds were made once we began, and then it was over and eradicated.

It's the whole causation vs correlation argument though - as it is all anecdotal and there's no real proof we had any effect on anything when it comes to the conventions of science. On a subtle energetic level though, that's a different story.

With the habitat of the kelip kelip, it's a bit more complicated on the human side. The encroachment is a mass of human desire all bundled into one energetic. From the clearing for agriculture and industry, to the dam. These things are huge and pressing with a momentum already in place. It's not like the killer algae, something that everyone wants gone. That's easy. The energy there is already moving in a direction of eradication and resolution, and all we had to do was boost it. Everyone loves fireflies, but people love money more.

All those thoughts rambling around in my brain mean nothing when actually doing the protocol, they just get in the way of what needs to occur, so I dropped them and went forward.

Over and over I sensed, described, and pushed the energy forward that this habitat and environment needed in order to stay balanced, and hopefully healthy. In my excursions inward, I sensed what needed to occur and it is truly a survival of this location in order to hold the kelip

kelip. There were some finer details coming through during these sessions on what could be done environmentally to support the habitat, but we had no real avenue anymore to affect that kind of nuts and bolts change.

What truly needs to happen is a wakeup call to people in this area. Shitting in your nest never turns out well, and this is not just about a species of fireflies, it is an ecosystem which is vital to the planet, and apparently beyond. Mangroves and salt marshes are overflowing with copious amounts of species in the early stages of life, so it's a huge birthing and feeding ground for many creatures. As well as that, these areas are known to clean the water of toxins and pollution we create; a filter for the planet. In most areas of the world, people have come to understand the extremely vital role they play within local and global economies, and have enacted laws to protect them. Not so here, and the fireflies are one of the main indicators there is a problem; the canary in the coal mine.

Since beginning the process of the EHP on this species and environment, there have been marked changes in how people are reacting to the environment and the fireflies along the Selangor River. There have been numerous conservation zones popping up all along the mouth of the river, and boat tours taking tourists to see the kelip kelip. It has become more and more, a large tourist destination that continues to grow. There does seem to be somewhat of a wake up around this, but because of the strong direction the place was already headed, it's like an aircraft carrier turning around... it takes a bit of time.

The dam itself has been problematic. In 2014, it inexplicably lost 40% of its water and no one is sure of the reason. There have been large tectonic shifts in the area, which could be attributed to the loss. As well, because of intense deforestation within Malaysia, the lake is filling with silt. Is the dam doomed? It may be.

In the whole scope of things, as far as complete resolution goes, there is no amazing rainbow at the end of the road, or even an end to the road. I feel the story of these firefly aliens breaching our earth and asking for help should result in a fantastic and amazing culmination of events, but it's just not so... at least not at this point, yet there have been small incremental changes. I just hope it's enough, and it keeps changing for the better.

John Vivanco

CHAPTER TWENTY-ONE
Project File -
The Strange Collection

"I've seen things you people wouldn't believe...."
  -Blade Runner

Putting my pen to the paper, I engage in the requisite squiggles and doodles to turn on the spigot where the images and senses flow. The table, the chairs, the room I am in, the sounds drifting in from outside, they all begin to wink out one by one until they are whispers, ghosts, nothing.

Seemingly inward I go, but in reality I am expanding and moving outside the limited perception of what is in front of me; going deep inside to see what is well beyond. You never know where you'll end up, where the "tasker" is going to send you. Anything, anywhere, any time; it's all game, I am blind to it, and have no notion of what I am to "see". My body begins to feel like it's vibrating and my mind is empty. I know this taste so well.

I feel like I am slipping down a rabbit hole and I begin to have immediate sensations of dust in my mouth. A lot of dust. Cascading words come to me, different temperatures touch my skin, my fingers dance over gritty surfaces. I write them all down as quickly as I can. I inhale deeply through my nose.

Dust.

My hands reach out as I move through the session, touching an angled surface jutting from a mound of red sand. Patting and groping the surface like a blind man I feel ridges and sand filled creases.

Ancient.

Brief images flit in and out, catching me by surprise and drawing me in while I am also trying to sketch them. Each sensation is like a lifeline pulling me deeper and deeper into the depths of this objective. Other Remote Viewers have sometimes called this, "chasing the signal line".

I just want to open my eyes.

Suddenly, without warning, I bi-locate

and I am there, wherever "there" is. I am in two places at once, at my desk and somewhere else, far, far away. At first it's like I have opened my eyes underwater where everything is shifting and oddly colored, but then it all snaps into place and I see clearly. I am standing in red sand. Red dust. I feel like it's hard to breathe and there's a terrible pressure in my head. Looming and monstrous artificial structures made of large stone blocks and covered in red dust crowd around me with the potential to blot out the sun.

The sun, what is it about the sun? It seems smaller, more distant ... dimmer than I am used to, and covered in a haze.

I shift my focus closer to an eroded pyramid shaped structure and the realization of an ancient civilization hits me. So ancient it feels slightly uncomfortable. I can put things into the context of human life and human civilization, from cave men on up to now, but this. This is beyond the human span of time in my experience and it creeps under my skin. I toss my pen down trying to rid this feeling and move on with my session.

More dust.

I drop and drift back down through the motes and haze, settling closer to this gargantuan structure. Where it rises out of the sand there are motifs, low relief designs, reminiscent of the Maya, reminiscent of the

Egyptians. Some kind of mysterious cuneiform dances around a massive collapsed entrance with fragments of columns littered about. Darkness spills outside and I can sense the ghosts still lingering in this place, flitting about the debris and shards of a long dead civilization.

In the early satellite imaging NASA conducted of the surface of Mars, there was an interesting anomaly, a land form that looked like a face. Around this formation were also what appear to be the edges of pyramid shaped forms. Of course it could all be pareidolia and the scientific community chalked it up as that, but many others did not. This was the first session I ever did on the mysterious Cydonia region of Mars, specifically what is known as that feature called "The Face".

When I received the disclosure on this objective, I was intrigued to say the least. From my own session on it, where I had a bi-location experience, it was clear to me these were ancient ruins.

I needed to dig deeper into this and so I began a project tasking the team of Remote Viewers on the same tasking I had done. If they too came back with the same information I had seen, then my plan was to map the region and other anomalies with remote viewing.

The basic question was non-leading and merely stated: "Describe the formation known as the "Face" in the Cydonia region of Mars" and I included a photo of the formation just to add the full intent.

One of the first things a Remote Viewer does when they get an impression of a structure in the beginning of their session is to identify right off, if it is artificial or natural - all of them determined it was artificial. Within their data, they included the same descriptions I had. Cuneiform, collapsed columns and structures so large it defies imagination. Pottery debris and shards littered everywhere on top of, and under the sand. To me, it was so astounding because we have been told for so long there's nothing there but the minds of crazy conspiracy theorists.

After that I began to map out the area, from what's currently there, who built them, what they looked like, what their culture was like, what happened to Mars, and inevitably them. It's a saga of epic proportions and so fascinating that my pen can't even begin to describe the reality of it.

The Cydonia region, in its biological heyday, sat on the edge of a vast ocean where plants, animals and humanoids lived and flourished. This was at least one of their cultural meccas and seats of power in the time they had. These Martians would often pilgrimage to this location during certain times of the year where some would, in a sense, "suicide" themselves, so they could be part of something greater. It's much like the stories we have from our ancient cultures about sacrificing a virgin to appease a god. In fact, a lot of the data we get back relating to the culture and symbols for these Martians, reminds Remote Viewers of ancient cultures on Earth. There are so many similarities that you really begin to wonder if they somehow had an impact on Earth cultures.

Mars went through an obvious geologic shift which decimated everything on the planet, and it happened rather quickly and violently. It appears, through remote viewing data, that it was twofold. An outside event which caused a massive energy wave knocked the planet off its axis and created a severe pole shift, quickly turning it into a completely desolate planet.

If you look at the satellite imagery that NASA has conducted on Mars, as well as the rovers that have imaged areas on the surface, there are quite a few anomalies which are either explained away or just shoved under the carpet. When you place the tool of remote viewing up against these you find that some are absolutely mundane, and some are truly unique.

My opinion is that Mars is littered with debris from this past civilization and NASA, among other agencies, know this as fact. I suppose, if it suits them to let us know this culture was there, then, and only then, will they let people know.

We have also conducted many remote viewing surveys into anomalies here on Earth and the Moon, whether it is of ancient origins (beyond the human scope of time) or UFO's. Sad to say, I have become part of that "virgin on their wedding night" crowd.

One curious planetary body is our Moon. This is another location littered with, not necessarily debris, but functioning bases. If people on Earth truly knew!

It's a difficult location to remote view, not because of issues with viewing it, but because of what can potentially take notice of you when you view it.

Like Mars, there are photos of the surface of the Moon, which show anomalies discounted or ignored by most. There have been numerous orbits by many craft in order to do this, one of which was Clementine. Interestingly, the satellite took 1.8 million images of the surface. Out of those images, 170,000 of them were made available to the public. The rest were classified. Classified moon craters?

At one point I was tasked blind on what appeared to be an anomaly in the Aristarchus Crater taken by the Clementine spacecraft in 1994.

For some strange reason I seem to have more bi-location events when a session deals with non-terrestrial locations. It may be there is a phenomena here to explore with regard to remote viewing. Perhaps there is a tighter focus and less "psychic noise" that can distract a Viewer. This particular session did not disappoint, yet it did get a bit dicey.

Running through the protocol you never really know what you're getting within a conceptual framework, and as such I was just cruising along when I dropped in to probe for some imagery.

Immediately when I did this, I found myself within what appeared to be a crater and fully lucid with a sustained visual where I could move around in a limited way. The walls of the crater were probably around 15 to 20 feet high, but I couldn't see outside of the crater to the horizon. I could see the immediate surface I was on as a fine gray dust, and the walls were somewhat crumbly. Like Mars, the atmosphere felt different and very thin, with a dark sky. The view I had was up against the crater wall, as well as an expanse within the crater itself. At this point the realization hit me that I was on the Moon.

In front of me, just off to my right, and inset into the crater wall, was an octagonal door surrounded within what appeared to be a metal framework. There was an inset handle of sorts within the door which looked like you were to spin it in order to open it up. Like a very large airlock door.

Deeper into the crater and the open atmosphere of the Moon there was activity occurring. A very difficult to describe scene lay before me, but it was like a clear bubble that ran over the top of part of the crater, and there were strange looking humanoids doing some type of work within it.

If you were to take a caper, the small green, wrinkled food item and turn it into something with arms and legs, that would be them. They seemed to be busy shuffling around and dealing with some moon related things that I have no idea about, when suddenly, "oh shit, they can see me!"

It was the heads turning towards me as well as the energy they put out which told me they knew I was there watching them, and that was not a good thing! I left as fast as I came and immediately tried to immerse myself in some mundane earth life event, like watching the Price is Right. I'm just a normal human here, nothing to see, please move along. I'm only interested in money and Vanna White, like all good Earth Humans. I did not want a visit from whatever these creatures were!

If you ask around in the remote viewing world, you will hear a lot of the same, but it's rarely talked about on the public side because of the danger. Ingo Swann, who was one of the godfathers of remote viewing, and part of the original CIA project, wrote a book called Penetration where he describes similar encounters and the danger surrounding it. In fact, one session he was asked to view a specific coordinate on the Moon, and it resulted in his handler stopping the session quickly, because he was noticed, just like I was.

We had some strange requests by people on the "inside" and they often dealt with matters that were in the realm of high strangeness.

One person we had worked with was at one point acting as a bridge and middleman to get us working with the FAA on many varied issues. This particular request though, was nothing mundane.

"I'm not supposed to talk to you about this, but someone is doing something experimental and I/we am/are concerned about it. Can you help?"

It's quite easy to task on that type of request because you just create the tasking around the "experimental" thing "they" are doing and then go from there.

It was blind viewing, blind analysis, and on top of that, it was something which was conceptually difficult to figure out. When you get into analysis on subjects you have no context for, like the realm of high strangeness, you will get congruent data from the Viewers but no way to relate it to anything in your world, and it can become difficult to explain.

Something extremely bizarre and scary was happening from this experiment, and he was right to be concerned. The Viewers described the ones conducting the experiment as not having a single clue about what they were unleashing or the implications, and they were doing it just because they could. The implications were so huge and far reaching, that it was dimension-wide.

This is where the data gets tricky though, as we can easily describe the emotional and far reaching implications, but what the hell is it?

"Combining things that should not be combined, and it's unleashing irreversible changes dimension-wide and through time". From what I could gather with the data, it appeared these scientists were playing with dimensions using a supercollider, or similar instruments. It's very exotic stuff, classified, and something the public is woefully unaware of.

It's like merging two dimensions or opening a door to a dimension that needs to stay closed and separated. It changes the basic fabric of our dimension in way that is completely wrong. Part of it is unseen and changes certain things that we aren't even aware of because it just becomes part of the fabric and it's as though we have always accepted it was that way. The other side of this is bringing something in from another dimension that should not be here, and it's not just one thing, it's many things. It would be like - from here on out, we are going to combine all human genes with crocodile genes and that's just the way it's going to be, but you won't even notice it.

We told him it was too late. It has been done, and can't be turned back. What else can you say?

CHAPTER TWENTY-TWO

Convergence Point

"Why the hell am I wearing these pajamas (my slang for the Zen meditation garb) all day? The sun is up, it's past noon, and I am sitting here in these god damned pajamas! OK, I have to get out of here. Oh hell, don't even mumble at me or look my way!! I am not in a good mood!"

That was the long and short of sesshin. All day, every day, 10 hours a day, for seven days. There would be times where I would be lost in the meditation, but mostly, I was tired, grumpy, and completely stupefied as to why I would even volunteer myself for this shit show so I could constantly battle myself. Because, really, that's what it comes down to. Just me.

If you want to come up against your basic human crap, go to sesshin. Because you will, no matter how peaceful you think meditation is.

A woman once asked me what I did and where I lived. When I told her, her eyes rolled back into her head in pleasure while her words slowed down into and a deepening tone like a record slowly coming to a stop, "It must be SOOOO peaceful".

It was like a rush stumble as I tried to quickly explain it was nothing of the sort, but her eyes had already glazed over and her brain had gone into fantasy land.

The perception of westerners on what it is like to live in a Zen center is quite often confused. It's either an idea of continual peace and serenity, as if you're sniffing flowers all day, or on the opposite spectrum, negative judgment on your apparent lack of contribution to society. "Damn navel gazers! You should be out making money instead of this selfish and narcissistic tomfoolery!"

After sesshin, it was always worth it. I always felt a deep silence, and for a brief moment I would not get as caught up in all the accumulated mental and emotional junk I had. I could begin to feel and live in a place where there is no suffering and I wanted to be there all the time. That's the thing with these intensives, it creates a situation in the moment where you are causing yourself suffering and you can't do anything about it. There are no distractions, just you looking at you, and you desperately wanting to be distracted by something - anything - because that's how we normally operate, chasing our desires and filling our voids. In everyday life, the moment I feel uncomfortable with a thought, feeling, situation... I shut down to the feeling of it and do something else. Sesshin creates a microcosm of our life and forces you into looking at you.

Aside from sesshin, people also came to the center three times a week to meditate, but beyond that I began to open up the zendo at 5am daily, for morning practice. It's not just on the cushion where meditation occurs but that seems to be the big focus in general. In order to really dig in deep, I knew I needed to practice all the time, whether I'm on a cushion or working through the day. It's about mindful action always, no matter the situation, but it's really easy to get lazy. Then again, it's my perception that I have to "do" something about all of it. The meditation crowbar. It's like trying so hard to pry open a can that can't be pried open, or even thinking there's a can there in the first place.

There were stories and warnings from those Zen elite, where they would admonish the ones who got caught up in tricks, which surfaced during long hours of meditation. Teachers regularly conduct what are called teishos, which are talks on Zen and the practice. They are meant to get us to go deeper and warn us of the pitfalls. Inspiration and fear.

A regular at the Zen Center for many years, one practitioner would always complain about this "propaganda", as she called it. I always thought that was hilarious. It seemed to be a holdover from some distant church related past she had. The job of the Zen teacher is not to fill someone up with any beliefs, it's to get you to practice more so you can let go of your beliefs. It's more garbage to let go of, but I was always annoyed with having to sit through those teishos, so I related on a certain level.

When you engage in a strong meditation practice, various phenomena can occur where you can get hung up. Telepathy, PSI, psychokinesis, seeing into other realms/dimensions, etc., and it can happen spontaneously. There are stories out there about people who began a practice and left because they came upon tricks and were excited about the potential of levitating, moving things with their mind, or any assortment of phenomena that keeps you hanging on.

It's just awareness opening and expanding, but often times it is easy to get caught up in endless cul-de-sacs, and instead of a practice of letting go, it becomes something else... an ego practice. There had been numerous occasions where I would hear other people's thoughts, could see and feel other people in other rooms, know things about people that I should not know ... etc., but I always worked to let go of that, and did not pursue it in those moments. At the same time I was working in remote viewing, and was always trying to deepen that – so in one sense, I felt I may be contradicting myself somewhat.

A conversation I had with a person who practiced alongside me was along the lines of, how people should not be doing remote viewing, and I shouldn't either. I and everyone else should only meditate, and I am doing a disservice to people by teaching it and talking about it on TV. This really pulled on my sense of the contradiction and guilt that I was already battling. I constantly played with the idea of dropping everything and focusing completely on the Zen side.

In reality though, the funny thing is, myself and everyone else have an infinite amount of things to get caught up in which keep us tied up in desires, so how is this any different? I think because it's perceived as a "special power" it could entice people. It's not a special power, it's part of a complicated biology and an aspect of who we are, if not proof that we are all one with everything. How could you remote view, if you all wasn't ONE? I am of the opinion that it is there, we all have it, so why would you hide from it?

I had also come to a totally different conclusion after battling and meditating with this. Amazingly, in the time that I began to sense there was no difference between RV and Zen,

Roshi said to me: "In order to be the best Remote Viewer you can possibly be, you have to let go of every shred of yourself so you can truly see what's there".

All roads lead to Rome. If you want to remote view, you have to let go, and that is all there is to it. When you remote view, you cannot have any ideas at all, and when you do come up with stories and ideas, you have to consciously let them go in order to see what's truly there. In a sense, you have to practice being empty. You can't know the reality of what you're viewing if you're making up stories about it. Same coin, different side. It's also what you do when you are engaged within a pure meditation practice.

Whether someone is on a spiritual path or not, and they have enough interest in remote viewing to receive training, you are teaching them to let go; the core of all knowing and spiritual practices.

The other side is how we ingest information from politicians, scientists, the news, or anyone who sets themselves up as an authority figure. The human population has a long history of being manipulated through ideas, and Remote Viewing can begin to shift this by providing the tools to know what is true and what is not true. It's not just by using the tool itself, it is what it turns on within the individual who begins to learn it. You begin to process information differently by sending it through your gut before your brain and you know when you're being lied to, even when it's a beautifully tied up information packet from CNN.

Lastly, there was the situation with the two week RV courses we served up, and the resulting increase in harassment from the covert group. They never wanted these to occur, and we knew the reason why. Within these classes, something greater took hold within each individual and the group mind. It caused a situation where people would "turn on" and this has the potential through a 100th monkey effect to change the world.

Overall, my drive to go back to a time before words, and to understand who I was, had created both my work life as well as my spiritual life. There was no difference between the two and all I was doing in a full time capacity, was practicing letting go, and bringing something to the world that could potentially change it.

This realization consolidated everything to one single point of focus, and I no longer felt conflicted about doing both Zen and RV, because they are one and the same. All I was doing was seeking the self and engaging in that process across all aspects of my life, no matter how it looked to someone on the outside.

But this letting go business... I really didn't understand what it meant at its core. I thought it to be just the act of forgetting in the moment so you don't hang on, and that's the way I was using it. It's almost like a compartmentalization skill, but still, the sense of self pervades and controls. What does it mean to really let go?

CHAPTER TWENTY-THREE
Project File - Quantum Financial Dilemma

Is it right and moral to increase the coffers and power of people with remote viewing? That was a lingering question when we began working in parts of the financial sector.

It's not that we were opposed to making money, but what does it mean to use this in order to know where financial markets are going so you can get rich or make someone else richer? Moral dilemmas for sure, but we also tread back into predicting the future and the issues surrounding that.

There were some big investment companies who took a sly interest in us, and greed seemed to ooze out of every pore with them. It was the same routine for the most part with a "pssst, hey, over here!" and a back door slightly ajar. When we were hired in this capacity we smelled all the greed, but shoved it to the background. At that moment we were more interested in figuring out how to test and use remote viewing in an area we hadn't ventured into yet.

There's a whole niche of remote viewing which focuses on a binary method of tasking to determine an outcome of an event, and it's often used in financial markets as well as betting on sporting events.

Very simplistically, the binary tasking method runs something like this: if team A wins then describe image A. If team B wins, then describe image B.

The tasker/analyst will have two images picked out which are very different from each other.

When you have a team of Remote Viewers working it, the analyst will collect their sessions and determine if the bulk of the sessions refer to image A, or to image B. The image most of the Viewers are describing will correspond to the team you will want to bet on. For the most part, it is similar within financial markets.

We found early on in our remote viewing experiments the success rate for tasking the binary method can be too low, so we didn't use it.

The Viewers will sometimes describe the wrong image very convincingly, and you will lose money on the wrong bet. Why would the Remote Viewer clearly describe the wrong image, the image for the losing team, and in such a way as to give you ultimate confidence?

For those who have ventured into this place and decided to walk away, some come to the conclusion that it is morally wrong and you're not supposed to do it, so that is why you have a strong error rate. For every person there is a different answer, but they often get the message that it just can't be done with accuracy.

In my opinion, none of it is morally wrong, that's an individual mental and moral construct. It's because from our 3D perspective, it will always be slightly inaccurate, and it has to do with the flow of time, dimensions, and impacts on the final outcome. Just like the constantly changing terrorist attacks, it goes back to the issue of remote viewing future events and what is demonstrated in the double slit experiment.

This goes for any tasking method on the future, not just binary methods, but binaries themselves can end up being less accurate. I believe the reason why conventional tasking is better here is because with the binary method you are trying to nail one single snippet in only one way. With conventional tasking methods, you are approaching the outcome from many different angles as opposed to just one. It can give you a clearer picture on the ultimate event, but it is not 100% and never can be.

I think people who try to predict outcomes would be better served if they tried to understand how consciousness affects the outcome, then work on that side of it. In other words – influencing the final outcome.

Over time though, the success rate on the winning side does average out over 50% on the binary method, but you need a betting plan to deal with the losses you will inevitably encounter. We needed to do much better than that for the financial companies immediately out of the gate.

One area we worked in were mergers and acquisitions -- if company A would merge with company B within a certain time frame. We would task on the outcome and analyze that. We would task on the emotional reaction of our investor to the outcome and analyze that. We tasked many, many different angles and added them up to come to a conclusion, and this worked much better than the binary method, to the point where we made some companies a hell of a lot of money. But it eventually collapses in on itself and you will get one or a series wrong. It all depends on when you want to end it.

It's not sexy work, and we never invested our own money in this. It wasn't that we were afraid we would lose, it just didn't feel right. We were using an amazing tool in order to make people wealthier than they already were, and that's a negative energy to be dealing with. We weren't solving problems and issues that needed care and attention, we were building the wealth and power for people who didn't need anymore.

John Vivanco

CHAPTER TWENTY-FOUR
Media and the EMP

I recall the first article on us. Somehow it leaked to the press, and the London Times was the first to report on psychic spies working for the FBI to stop terrorist attacks. I have no idea where the leak came from, but it was all about our company, and it made me nervous.

We were popular within the Remote Viewing world, so much so that we drew in a lot of first time students, and subsequently each class we conducted was full. We were not so popular, though, with the ex-military remote viewing trainers and the people close to them. This was due to the fact that we were not in the ex-military club and we would constantly change things within the remote viewing protocol. There was, and still are, arguments within the "community" on whose protocol is better. You don't even need a protocol as you can just tap in to "see" what's there! It's manufactured tension and the creation of "sides", which is why I always stayed away from it. I find it strange Remote Viewers would fall into that trap. They are supposed to be intuitive and sensitive, but I suppose we all have our blind spots.

Nonetheless, we were concerned it would create some upset within the upper echelons of the RV community, and even more of a worry, enrage, even more, the covert group attacking us.

Before we could respond to any requests from the media, we had to get clearance from the FBI. I thought they would say no, or maybe I was hoping... but that wasn't the case. Of course they also said that they would neither confirm nor deny they were working with us, when approached.

One of the most important things to me, and what I believed in, was the work we were doing and what it could do for the world, so I wanted to keep my head down in order to keep doing it. More often than not, everything felt contentious surrounding us. From the verbal attacks on our character and mudslinging within the RV community, to the covert group attacking us. Add to that, an exponential jump about to occur on the side of a society who is taught that this stuff is fake, we were about to be attacked on all sides now. Of course, clients and students would roll in, which is good, but I wanted the media appearances to happen without me in them.

Unfortunately, it wouldn't. I am directing operations and running it all with Pru; and being one of the top Viewers, I had to be on camera to demonstrate. There was no other choice.

With every media request we got, we vetted it by remote viewing the outcome for us, and we turned down quite a few because of this. If there were any indication we would not be treated fairly, we declined it.

One interview was for *CBS Sunday Morning*, where I and another Viewer remote viewed an objective they chose. In the session, I had a subject in a city area, wearing a lot of wool as well as a large hat. The subject seemed to have a very strong paraphysical aspect moving around his body, which was akin to a death or dying state.

The other Viewer on this objective with me had the same general information and was also explaining how something slammed into and killed him. While we were remote viewing and describing out loud our impressions, you could hear gasps from the interviewer and the camera operator. They were impressed and convinced by it.

It turns out the objective they chose was the moment Abraham Lincoln was assassinated.

Our data reflected this, but once the final piece aired, the host said we will never know if it's real or not. What a way to engineer thought.

What it comes down to, aside from keeping people in a state of doubt, is the belief we have to place it in context and name it. The problem is, we don't do that in remote viewing because it's not considered "data", and is mostly useless to the analyst - in other words, it's typically wrong. People watching TV don't understand the remote viewing protocol, and if one of us deducted an event that was not the assassination of Lincoln, that would have been bad for us because everyone would say - they were wrong! In remote viewing, you just describe what you are receiving and stay away from high level concepts.

There were many media outlets, from TV to print, both locally and internationally, and through it all, I could feel danger coming from this attention we were receiving. One thought was, what if the terrorists came after us? I had read Al Qaeda made a statement about us, that we are of the Djinn and evil, so there was a possibility some lone actor could try to kill us, but there was also no indication this would happen. Occam's Razor - like in the past - the real danger lies with the covert group who wants us out of this business altogether.

Because of all the terrorist work, we were sitting on a huge trove of information.

Information very few people knew. We knew how these nukes worked, what they looked like, how the bio/chem agents worked, what they were going to use, where they were getting it, where they were going to do it, and on and on. Every single bit of information, both reports and raw data, were relayed to the FBI as we worked through it in real time.

In the deep background, while the media influx is heaving full force, and we are working ourselves to the bone, the danger became immediately apparent.

Because of the Patriot Act we traded an amount of "freedom" for "security", which infinitely pleases people who want to remain in power and control. A government's main purpose, is in fact, to keep power and control. It gives them more avenues to abuse their power and broader authority to screw with those that don't agree with them, or whom they don't like. That presented an opportunity for the covert group whose operation was to get rid of us.

We were warned from the inside, the potential we were going to get raided because of all the information we had. We could be painted as terrorists of a sort, shut down and potentially locked away. We were doing nothing wrong at all, just fulfilling their request, and thought we were doing the good and right thing in helping our country and saving lives. It was inconceivable to me someone would even try and bum-rush us like this. I shook my head at the incomprehensibility of this as I began the process of eliminating as much of it as I could, from data files, to sessions, to notes and reports, and somehow we dodged that bullet. After this incident, we began the process of slowly separating ourselves from this work. It was clear the danger was reaching a new level and we could eventually run into something worse... death.

The media attention seemed to go out with a bang as well. The Sunday London Times wanted to come out and spend a week with us taking photos and interviewing us for an insert they had in their paper. It's not TV, but it's a multi-page spread with color pictures, and for some reason it felt safe to do.

We had a two week training course coming up so we pulled them into the class and brought in all of our professional Viewers so they could get interviewed and involved. The best way to explain to the press what Remote Viewing is, was to immerse them in a class. Because we had remote viewed the outcome and decided to accept, we knew it would be part of the factor in creating a positive piece on us.

You can be hoodwinked by the media, as they have an agenda and opinions they want to push forward. Positive interviews can often turn into bat shit crazy after the editor finishes the job. Fortunately for us, we knew the writer to be interested in this, and it seemed the British in general had an insatiable appetite for it as well.

The Sunday Times crew took photos, interviews, learned RV and built their piece. They were impressed by what the other students went through and they themselves had some good moments learning the process. Unfortunately, they left just a couple of days before the real fun started.

When you try to explain to someone you're being followed, your house is bugged, they want to kill us, and a whole host of other dastardly things being brought on by some nameless and unknown government spooks, it doesn't go so well. The media loves this, and that's why we would not bring it up. They love it from the standpoint of, "these guys are crazy, let's play it up", and that gets ratings for them, which is their only interest.

With The Times, we were a bit more open than with other media outlets. For one, they were taking the class, which places them in a vulnerable position; and two, they believed in it already. We explained some of the intrigue and death threats and it always begs the question of why? It's very difficult to say you don't know why when you're a Remote Viewer, but we often did. To the world out there, it was declassified and that means the government does not care about it, so what's the point in trying to stop us?

What I found entertaining at times is when we would speak of some of this to students, or others within the remote viewing community, and they would ask an ex-military Remote Viewer about it. "Do you guys get harassed and death threats like those other guys do"? They'd come back to us and say, "I asked so and so about it and they said that kind of stuff doesn't happen". It's like asking the wolf guarding the sheep if he's going to eat you.

It was the last day of the two week class when it went a bit strange.

The class was located in an office building off a main highway in a business area of Carlsbad. The complex was a couple of office buildings split by a small road coming off the highway. In all, there were four very large glassy boxes facing each other with a parking lot dividing them.

We were in one of these buildings on the second floor, and it was deserted, except for us and our class. There was a reception area with couches and chairs where I was hanging out with the professional Remote Viewers, in all there were five of us there. Pru was down the hall with the students at that moment in the small room with no windows which served as our classroom.

We had often come here in the past, not for classes, but for meetings with clients. It was a quiet and professional location for that, but a two week class bent the patience of everyone who actually worked there. Crazy remote viewing people with media coming and going all day every day. In order to stay away from there as much as I could, I conducted a separate and advanced training for the professional Viewers, while Pru mostly took care of teaching the beginning class. When we needed to help with the beginning class, or get interviewed and interact with The Times people, we would head to the class location.

With no other office workers to bother us on the weekends, and it being the last weekend, we were all there.

On the last day we usually have students come up with a tasking for the professional Remote Viewers to view. This gave them a chance to task us on something cool they all agree upon, practice tasking methods, watch us view it, and see what our sessions look like. While they worked on creating the idea of what we are to remote view and pulled the tasking together, we left the room.

We headed to the lobby area, just down the dark hallway and waited around for them to finish up and let us know when to begin viewing for them. While waiting for this, about five minutes passed, and then all hell broke loose.

The power died, and with that fire doors started closing, accompanied by a screeching alarm throughout the whole building. As the doors were closing, we all scrambled to get on either side, fearing being trapped in a dark hallway with no exit, or by the windows and emergency stairs.

My only thought was, "this is it, they are finally making good on the death threats, and coming to kill us". I feared for the students in the – likely - pitch black room, but I had to see if anything was coming our way first instead of running to them. The others seemed to catch wind of this and we all crouched as we made our way to the window to look out over the parking lot. I knew there was an emergency staircase to the left and I sent another team member to keep watch while I scanned the parking lot for the approach of men with guns. I fully expected the jig was up, and this was the end.

Watching from the window, not much was happening in the lot, so a couple of the professional Viewers decided to run back to the classroom and check if everyone was OK. I met up with the person watching the stairs and we carefully and slowly made our way down. Our intent was to get out to the parking lot and beyond, so we could figure out what was happening. As I made my way out I saw nothing out of the ordinary, so I decided to hang back and wait while the other Viewer ran across the lot. While waiting, I decided to go to the other office buildings across the small road. Perhaps there would be an indication of a power outage that would explain what was happening in our building. There was obviously no fire.

As I came to the road, there were a number of cars at a dead stop in the middle, and a few people walking around with confused looks on their faces. That was a curiosity, but I kept moving to the other buildings. There were very few people around on this Sunday afternoon, but I found a security guard who told me the power was out in all the buildings, and he did not know why.

Making my way back to the office building, I stopped and spoke to a person standing outside their car. They explained they were just driving along and out of the blue their car went dead in the middle of the road. The other drivers in this situation had the same story.

Once back in our building, I walked up to our floor to see some of our team standing around. Pru was still in the classroom speaking with the students, so I began to tell them what I saw. As I was relaying this, Pru came out somewhat livid. "Do you know what they did!? They were going to task us on the biggest secret of the Stargate program!" The Stargate program was what the CIA had declassified, and subsequently RV itself. Apparently the students had five different objectives they were running through and voting on, for us to remote view; the moment they came to a consensus we were to view the biggest secret, is when the power went out.

There were a couple of occasions in the past where we had inadvertently remote viewed something classified. Like anyone else, we are curious people, but with some projects we did on the more esoteric side, we would sometimes step on toes. Stuff that exists within the mythology and the annals of conspiracy theories, you wouldn't think is classified, we sometimes viewed. Afterward a message would be delivered in an off-putting way, a bizarre and unexplainable event on the surface. We would view the event to understand it and then make some kind of veiled apology that we wouldn't do it again.

Unfortunately, the students had no idea of any of this, and the confirmation of this being a message came in the form of a confused utility worker.

There was a large green utility box where the power of the buildings routes through on the side of the road. A utility worker had shown up to figure out what went wrong there, and get it fixed. As we approached, he was scratching his head, so we asked what happened. He explained: "this is impossible, this can't happen. All the circuits, everything in here is fried, totally gone. There is not nearly enough power routing through here to fry this box and the only way it can happen is if it came from the outside".

The implication based on the timing, the deduction from the utility worker, and the fact that a bunch of cars were dead on the street lead me and everyone else to believe it was an intentional EMP.

John Vivanco

CHAPTER TWENTY-FIVE
The Breakdown

Most of the things in my life that meant something to me were gradually dissipating and drying up. My marriage was in shambles, and on the brink of ending with no real way to fix it. I was going one way and she was going the other.

As you unravel yourself and look deep inside, you also begin to "not" engage in the dysfunctions that take you into relationships, or a relationship. Quite often the reason you got involved in the first place was based on two people's dysfunctions working together and keeping things dysfunctionaly status-quo. For me, I had seen it with amazing clarity, and I wanted to change myself, for myself. The problem is, if the other is unwilling to see and change then the connection dies, because the reason for the relationship is no longer there.

My aloofness within the relationship was directly related to the fear I had of loss. If I could stay aloof, then I would not feel the pain when it's over, which is a self-fulfilling prophecy. For her my aloofness played into her sense of low self-esteem, and she needed that in order to preserve the idea of who she was. I was moving in the direction of cleaning that up within myself, and the reflection on the marriage was me trying to be involved and fully present with her. I found it interesting she would turn the opposite direction from that, as if it propelled her away.

On the other side of that, I'm a pain in the ass to be with for a number of reasons. With wild gesticulations and passionate ramblings, I can soapbox the hell out of things that get me riled, then glide back into being unaffected and calm. If I find a path I want to go in, which often runs counter to what others want of me, I'll still do it because I'm stubborn and headstrong. I'll also float around in my head for long periods of time with no communication or thought of what's occurring around me. Just locked away trying to figure something out or accomplish a goal without much communication.

Whenever she was home, which became less and less frequent, I could feel the anger coming from her. She was building up something intense and what really killed me was how it was affecting our son. It was the two of us combined, and we were both responsible for it. One moment I could clearly see what was going to happen and felt OK with it, the next, I was an emotional wreck.

My son, Sebastian, and I were buddies, and he was my main light. Working at home and taking care of the Zen Center, I was Mr. Mom. We would practice remote viewing together and run around the inside of the zendo. I would ask him, "Ok, remote view Grandpa and tell me what he's doing right now". He would close his eyes for a moment straining to grab a visual, and then frustratingly exclaim, "Grandpa is eating the Cheetos again! He always eats ALL the Cheetos!" I would die laughing and then send him off onto another remote viewing foray. From hiding his favorite stuffed animal and getting him to perceive where it was, to perceiving what the coolest thing happening at Disneyland in that moment. The kid was a natural, and aside from that, he and I have always had a very strong telepathic connection, knowing what the other is thinking. He says what I think, and I say what he thinks.

On the other side of my marriage coming apart, TDS was crumbling as well. All the years of harassment and destruction of our business ventures by a covert group had taken its toll. Our company assets were frozen by the IRS because, as they said, "we want you to tell us who has invested in you, it could be a drug dealer, and that is illegal". This was none of their business as we were incorporated in Nevada where that information is private. They also knew who was funding us because we couldn't make a any move without them knowing, and it was just another tool the covert group was using in order to sink us. We had lawyers eventually free it up, but then our investor was warned by someone in political office that they should not be messing with this, and especially us. Shortly after, the investor was blackmailed into pulling out.

At this point we were practically broke, with no way to pull enough money in, even though we were still cruising off the wind of publicity around our counter-terror work. The more that came our way, the more we had to dodge on the side of harassment, and the more we felt we would either be killed or finally fall to one of their setups. We had plenty of Viewers always willing and able to do the work, but the danger started to spread to them as well. It appeared that was the last line, because we wanted to protect them.

Being completely decentralized we had to use electronic communication for everything, which was our Achilles heel. Early on we would use PGP encryption in every email, but that was pointless in the face of our computers being hacked. We had a couple tiers of people, from Pru and myself, then the professional Viewers, the interns after that, and finally the catchall group. The last group would get fairly large, because once someone took a class from us they could drop into it if they wanted to continue with more training and engage in interesting projects.

Occasionally we would task this larger group to see how they were doing and look for any standouts, or find unique ways people were viewing, when we took notice of something strange happening.

No matter what they were tasked on, the sessions we were getting back were just not right. It was as though there was another layer of information over the tasking that we had written up for them. Information which was congruent between sessions, but not in the least bit related to what we had tasked, and this was something we hadn't run into before. Being a bit alarmed by this we needed to figure out what was happening.

By remote viewing the issue, it was clear to see that the sessions were getting intercepted electronically and then re-tasked on something else. In other words, we have what we want the Remote Viewer to view and we write it up with a directive (DIR:) and tag[2], then send that to them via email which looks somewhat like this:

DIR: SFJ-99
Tag: 3489 5003

After they receive that, they run through

---

[2]A "directive" is the session identifier and used for filing purposes. The tag is the random eight digit number, much like a coordinate, that the Viewer uses to access the objective/target. A Viewer only receives these two items, and not the actual description of what they are to remote view. That is omitted before and held by the person tasking the Remote Viewer.

the protocol and send us their session.

Unknown to us, the Directive (DIR) and Tag we send out for every session was intercepted and someone else would assign a totally different objective/target to it. It screws with the data you get back because it adds other layers of information within the sessions. One incredible thing we found with our experimentations around this, is a Remote Viewer will actually try and describe multiple taskings on one single directive and tag. In other words, within their data, you can align information from multiple (and very different) questions. Nonetheless, from an analyst's point of view it's problematic, because it can really screw with the conclusions you need to come to.

The more insidious side of this, rather than just screwing with data, was our Viewers could be tasked on things which could destabilize them over time. For instance, what would it do to the mind of a Remote Viewer if they were constantly tasked on something extremely negative, session after session, and they never knew about it? This was the main issue for us. We could add more intent in the taskings, for instance adding - "only view the tasking from TDS", but it was just a band-aid, because when you plug one hole they will open another one. We were also very worn out by all the death threats, surveillance, setups, and the general bashing, so we didn't have the energy to keep fighting and reorganize in a different way.

In my Zen practice I was completely engaged in the routine, as I had been for a long time, but there was a sense I was running out of time. An urgency seemed to come out of nowhere and I couldn't pinpoint what it was, other than a looming death. It was disconcerting, but I knew sometimes these feelings could be metaphorical rather than literal, and it could merely mean I would be leaving the Zen Center.

Waking up before dawn every day, sitting long hours, I was tired, and it seemed like I was up against an endless wall. At the same time there were those points of silence and peace that would keep me digging as deep as I could. I also knew there was absolutely nothing I could do, and nowhere else I could go. In my life, the only important avenue is to know the self; it's my only job, my only career. I knew with just the practice of the meditation, all beings benefit in ways seen and unseen, so I had to keep going.

With this feeling of no time left, I began to get a slowly forming cold. It's one of those your kid brings home from school, and even though it was a simple head cold, it had a slightly different quality to it. The typical cold for me would be a stuffy and thick nose dripping down the back of my throat on occasion that eventually goes away. The difference with this one was the faucet was dripping and going into my lungs. I would seem to get over it after a week or two and then it would come back after a week. I was healthy and exercised, so it seemed strange this would linger.

When I went to the doctor I wasn't feeling too bad. I never had a fever with this, just slightly rundown and coughing. He thought perhaps there was a bit of walking pneumonia, prescribed some antibiotics, and told me it should be gone by the time I ran out of them.

As if to drive a point home that this was not normal, the moment I started taking antibiotics was the moment this thing decided to blossom. A fever took over which was a writhing, nasty, achy hell that no amount of aspirin could wrangle to the ground, and on the night of the second day of this I began to drift in and out of a lucid and startling fever vision.

I saw a monk from the deep past, draped in gold and red, as he laid in the repose of death upon an altar. There was incense wafting and trailing in the darkened candle lit atmosphere around him, as other monks chanted his spirit into the afterlife. The sounds of the chanting were vibrating the stringy smoke of the incense as it moved over him and upward to the ceiling of this ancient temple, which was in Nepal.

The monk had spent his life within the temple and he was in his 30's when he passed. When I saw him I immediately understood the relationship to me. He was me, and his death was by pneumonia.

I was pulling on a deep memory. It's like

when you hear a song you haven't heard in years, one that you loved, and brings up memories of that time, memories you thought were lost forever. My pneumonia was the song that brought this memory back.

He faced a choice at that moment in time in his life. He had spent a life in meditation and had some openings but the opening his soul was seeking had not come yet. At the point where his life path needed it to happen within a physical existence, he could not do it. There was a leap of faith he had to take, but it wasn't in him because of mental attachments to the simple desires he had, even after living in a monastery for such a long time. So he had to die.

In the life I lead right at this moment, I realize I am again at the same crossroads of choice, and I was indeed running out of time.

John Vivanco

CHAPTER TWENTY-SIX
The Phoenix

Just let go.

Just let go.

Just let go and die.

Somehow I can't, because I don't know how, or what it means.

It feels as though I am on the head of a pin, fully exposed and being torn to shreds mentally, physically and spiritually. Laying inside a small hut in the mountains of New Mexico I can see an airplane through the skylight, the only place I want to be is on that plane and out of this torment. This Zen Monastery.

Within the mountains of New Mexico, above Santa Fe, the winters get cold and snowy. Temperatures reach the 30's in the day and single digits at night. I had to come here on a somewhat regular basis for Zen training and especially sesshin, where we would meditate for a week, and this time it was in the dead of winter.

The small adobe structure was made from the mud of the surrounding land, and an intense and deep quiet pervaded this place. A quiet that tears you apart. The zendo itself was small, able to accommodate about 10 people, with a couple of bunk rooms inside the main structure where the zendo was. Outside, there was an outhouse and two small 12 x 12 structures, one of which was a bare bones kitchen, and the other used for storage.

The days were long, intense and difficult here. Notable and un-notable all in the same breath. I had been to many of these already, spanning from three days to a week, sometimes even back to back sesshin, but they didn't seem to get any easier.

Like any sesshin, every moment, aside from the brief rest periods, is completely structured, and you slowly grind through it. They are designed to be a pressure cooker where you look closely and deeply at yourself. You are exhausted from lack of sleep, your body hurts from 8 to 10 hours of sitting - unmoving - daily, you have to use an outhouse in the snow, you are cold most of the time, you can't talk, you have to meet with your teacher three times a day in a private interview, all meals are formal ceremonies, and the days are endless.

Each person is in their own private heaven or hell, but mostly hell, and often times will begin to display small bits of acting out. "The placement of these objects I brought with me has to be in a certain configuration just next to where I sleep, yet you can't just put them in random order. They have to be cycled out into different positions nightly before bed ... and in doing this, it upholds the Universe and I won't die". That would be a very small example of a clinging and acting out I witnessed from another practitioner. It's all geared to keep a sense of identity intact, and I get it - I am in the same boat.

It's like the last line of defense, the last battlefront you guard and try to keep safe. If you go through enough of these sesshin, those ramparts can hopefully fall, revealing something entirely different and astounding, a new way to see, a new way to live. This is a leap of faith you have to take to get there, and in the moment of taking it, it's the most difficult thing in the world to do. My acting out to keep from this, was the conspiring of how to leave, and also finding unique hiding places during rest periods which somehow felt as though I was preserving some aspect of myself from getting torn up.

Sesshin in the winter and the snow makes it all the more difficult. In the early morning or during the late night meditation, Roshi would open the doors of the zendo to the single digit temperatures. The cold air would take over, dropping it down so the outside was the same as the inside. We needed to move past that as we sat there unmoving and generate our own heat. When you meditate you can find a place within so it does not affect you, and in fact, you can generate enough heat within yourself where the snow and ice melt around you. Fortunately, we didn't have to go that far.

It was cold, but it didn't bother me nearly as much as what was going on internally.

To the self (or your identity), an ego death is a taken as a physical death, and it's the one place it does not want to go. It clings to any shred of self-identity and any affront to it, which means that it fights like you wouldn't believe. My brain was telling me I am dying, and there was a battle going on to stay alive. Even though I had my places to hide from it all, it was not working. Emotions, thoughts, situations to cling to kept popping up in violent and surprising ways.

In my hiding place on the breaks as I stared through the skylight above me, I would physically writhe with the death I knew was coming. At the basic level, I just wanted out of here. Why? Because I am afraid. Afraid of losing my wife, my son, my work. Afraid of losing me.

But hell, it's all going away anyway and there's not much I can do. The pneumonia I had was there in the background, staved off somewhat but ready to come roaring back to kill me and I knew it. But thoughts would come, telling me I can save the marriage and the business of TDS, I have to save it and I have to get out of here right now in order to do that. So I am doomed either way; death here or death there. What if I didn't care, would it make it easier? But again, what does it even mean to let go, and how do I do it?

Roshi said me, "Why do you keep sticking your hand in the fire when you know it will burn you?" I repeated the words in my head over and over trying to understand. The fire are my desires but how do I not do that? It's like asking a person born without eyes to just see. How can you see when you don't even have the faculty for it. It's not built in, it's not part of a nature you think you have. It seems that all I have is desire and chasing it down in every moment of my life. Products, relationships, thoughts, feelings... one breaks or is uncomfortable and I look to fill it with a new one.

It was a battle with Mara, the one who entices with ideas and desires that are wholly mundane and irrelevant when you are in the midst of completely letting go. I knew this was also the battle people go through once they slip out of the body and die. Whatever deep desires you have can catapult you back into a mundane human life and all the suffering it brings. We want out of this suffering so bad, but are unwilling to make that leap when it comes right down to it. This is where I was left, having to make some kind of leap but not knowing how to do it or where it goes.

The days seemed like forever, mixed with an eternal silence that gave way to an intense panic that I was going to die. A back and forth mental hell. Then it struck me in its simplicity. Don't stick your fucking hand in the fire! No matter what, just stop focusing on what is causing the pain.

As I practiced slipping past the churning desires and moving to a place of deep meditation an errant thought and feeling kept coming up. I kept pushing it away in the belief I had to focus and not succumb to any vision or thought which would drive me out of what I believed I had to do. Because it would not leave me alone, I decided it must be important so I brought it into focus.

It was the fifth day, and early in the morning when I let myself drift into this. Quietly sitting on my cushion, I tugged just a bit and a whole scene was waiting right there for me. I was a young boy at school in the first grade. The old linoleum floor had small rocks and sand tracked in by the kids, and would make a scraping noise that seemed excruciatingly loud every time I moved my chair and feet, while the voices of the other kids sounded like fingernails on a chalk board. I was overwhelmed with the sounds, textures, feelings and pressure of this place. I could also sense all the emotions of everyone in the classroom. It was like a cacophony of jumbled and chaotic feelings coming from everywhere at once, which caused immense fear and panic inside me.

I was sitting at my desk, completely involved in practicing my new writing skills when the teacher angrily lurched forward and grabbed my left hand. As she clenched it tightly, she told me I must never, ever write with the left hand. She said I must always use my right hand, and forced me to do something that went completely against my nature.

Not that I understood any of this at the time, but she must have been an ex-Catholic nun, and on the cusp of generations, between the Middle Ages and now! There used to be the notion that the "right hand is of god" and "the left hand is of the devil", so children who were left-handed were forced to use their right, lest they fall into the clutches of Satan. She somehow made her way into modern day public schools with this in tow, and unwittingly sent me down a lifelong struggle because of it.

I was feeling all of this as if it were happening again. All of the overwhelming fear, frustration and indignance, yet wanting to please the teacher at the same time. One moment, pure open exploration, the next moment shut down with fear by someone who I was supposed to look up to.

When that happened I immediately split and stepped back behind the teacher and the little boy within me, where the scene replayed itself. This time I was the grown-up mixed with a very deep compassion and understanding, but there was something else. I was me, but I also felt like I was Avolkitesvara, the Bodhisattva of Compassion. All I could do was hold the scene of the boy and the teacher in love and compassion... just hold it with no judgments.

I could see the boy in all his fear and indignance, and in that single moment, form a self-identity with rebellion of authority at its core. The teacher had no idea what she was doing, she was just running on a script she had. A misunderstanding through ignorance and being unaware, but there is nothing I could feel but compassion for her, for the little John, for all the kids there.

My life then began to flash before my eyes. All the moments where there was an intense emotion occurring, a troubling circumstance, and my reaction and deed toward it. All the moments I affected people in my life, and myself, in a negative or positive fashion unfolded. Fighting and rebelling against everything, hurting significant people in my life because of an emotional ineptitude and not wanting to see it within me.

The whole point of my life led to this moment where I clearly see that Zen is going against the grain, it's a rebellion. Art school and bands are a rebellion. Remote Viewing and what it's for bucks up against authority structures. Being involved passionately with these are all coming from a script I created. It's a self-identity and a belief of who I am.

As it all streamed past my mind's eye, it came to a dead stop at the moment of now. In a space of complete silence where no words and ideas can exist, just the immense unfolding of what is, is where I sat.

In this I saw there is no chasing anything, because there is nothing to chase.

There is no "me" to chase anything, only emptiness.

Yet within this emptiness all form arises.

All the thoughts and ideas are just clouds appearing and dissipating.

This "I" is a cloud forming and dissipating. It's there and not there, and there is nothing to hold onto.

There is no suffering, there is no death, there is no truth, there is no searching.

No more searching.

It's right here and it's always been right here.

I have been screaming I am dying of thirst while living on the banks of a beautiful clean river to drink from.

I am all things at once and yet there is nothing. There is only THIS, and everything is perfect.

The time before the secret words is where everything lives, breathes and dies in one unadulterated, unfolding moment. It's before thought and the creation of a self-identity. I spent a life unraveling myself so I could see what Mr. Causey meant by this and it was the greatest gift I could ever receive.

Uncontrollable tears were streaming down my face and when the bell rang and I removed myself from the cushion, a joy unlike any joy came forth, attached to nothing. It just was.

There were things to do like walking, breathing, listening to the snow fall, feeling the cold on my skin, and watching the icicles melt, so I had to get to it.

Where does life go from here?

Allowing the ideas that created the physical construct of my life circumstances to dissipate. Placing one foot in front of the next, watching the sunset, feeling the pain of a broken relationship, or a crushed business, hearing the song of a bird or the roar of a bulldozer, and being with whatever there is and whatever I feel. I can do whatever I want.

About the Author

After Pru and John closed TDS, John began working on projects surrounding remote viewing and television for National Geographic. Of the belief that remote viewing has the potential to change the world, John's endeavors have focused more on the public side, even though he still takes on the occasional client.

His current undertakings involve running a team under righthemispheric.com, where they work on a variety of projects from the esoteric to the mundane. As well, he continues to film and work with a producer around his remote viewing projects. A big proponent of - not being an armchair Remote Viewer – much of his work has to do with investigations, and the lining up of data out in the field. An adventure always awaits!

Aside from TV and writing, you can find John teaching classes on remote viewing, as well as the occasional radio interview and conference.

i   Double Slit Experiment - If you take a panel with a single slit and shoot marbles through it, the obvious occurs, a pattern on the back wall in the form of the slit the marbles went through. If you use water instead of marbles and send a wave through the single slit, the same pattern, like the marbles, is created on the back wall - just a single line.

Something different happens when you use two slits instead of one. Of course, when you shoot the marbles through, two patterns emerge on the back wall in accordance with the slit patterns, because that is how matter acts.

With waves though, once the single wave passes through the two slits, two wave forms are created. As they spread out, the top of one wave will meet the bottom of another wave, which cancels them out, and you will get what's called an interference pattern. This results in varying bands of light and dark across the back wall, as opposed to just two bands with the marbles. That is the difference between how a particle and a wave act in very rudimentary terms.

In the same experiment, when you take a photon, which is a tiny particle, like a marble, quantum strangeness rears its head.

When you shoot the photon through one slit, it behaves like the marble and you get a single slit pattern on the back wall. When you have two slits, you would expect the pattern on the back wall would be two slits, but you don't. You get an interference pattern with many bands, so the photon acts like a wave and a particle at the same time.

The single photon is a particle, but it becomes a wave of possibilities, then goes through both slits and interferes with itself to create the interference pattern. It, in fact, goes through all the possibilities of what could occur as opposed to just one. This is a contradiction to the human mind and impossible, but on the quantum level it is not.

If there is an observer to the event where the photon passes through the slit in the exact same experiment, it will change its behavior yet again. The observation on a quantum level causes the photon to behave like a particle and not a wave when passing through 2 slits. Consequently the pattern on the back wall is only two slits because the wave function collapses.

Made in the USA
Middletown, DE
09 August 2020

14912394R00155